RICHARD CRANE: RUSSIAN PLAYS

Richard Crane

# RUSSIAN PLAYS

from original translations by
Faynia Williams

**Brothers Karamazov**

**Vanity**

**Gogol**

**Satan's Ball**

OBERON BOOKS
LONDON

WWW.OBERONBOOKS.COM

First published in this collection in the United Kingdom in 2011
by Oberon Books Ltd
521 Caledonian Road, London N7 9RH
Tel: 020 7607 3637 / Fax: 020 7607 3629
e-mail: info@oberonbooks.com
www.oberonbooks.com

Visit www.oberonbooks.com to read more about all our books and to buy
them. You will also find features, author interviews and news of any author
events, and you can sign up for e-newsletters so that you're always first to
hear about our new releases.

# Contents

*to Faynia*
*who made these plays with me*

# BROTHERS KARAMAZOV

'Deservedly the box office hit of the official Festival... *Brothers
Karamazov* is a total triumph...'
Jack Tinker, *Daily Mail*

'A theatrical experience of magnitude, both exciting and
exhilaratingly thoughtful... The famous encounter between
the ancient priest and Jesus is staged with that same intensity
and flamboyance which have won the Crane-Williams team
awards for five previous productions on Edinburgh's Fringe...'
John Barber, *Daily Telegraph*

'Richard Crane's version of *Brothers Karamazov*... is a gripping,
intelligent, strongly acted, two-hour chamber-work that seizes
on the family drama as a microcosm of the turmoil in Russian
society...'
Michael Billington, *The Guardian*

'This Brighton Theatre production hits the jackpot... With
emphasis on the usually suppressed comedy, Mr Crane paves
the way for a full explosion of Slavic fervour in the prosecuting
lawyer's speech...'
Irving Wardle, *Times*

'An attempt to compress and distil the essence of
Dostoyevsky's towering masterpiece within two hours... is
like climbing Everest in dancing-shoes... Richard Crane's
adaptation for Brighton Theatre... is an ingenious miniature,
conveying both the scale and scope of the original...'
Nichols de Jongh, *Guardian*

'Superlative... fascinating... a brilliant distillation... Where the
RSC's *Nicholas Nickleby* tackles a great novel with sound and
fury and a cast of fifty, this does it with stealth and implication
and a cast of four...'
Sheridan Morley, *Punch*

# VANITY

'Richard Crane's glittering diamond of a play... a rare
theatrical treat...'
*Time Out*

'The drama unfolds at speed, from the sardonic opening to
a breath-taking tragic climax... Faynia Williams directs with
brilliance...'
*Glasgow Herald*

'...Crane moves into social and psychological territory
unvisited by Tchaikovsky... he varies the theatrical couplets
with ironic shifts of tone, occasionally going into prose
and pointing up the characters' inner lives with brutally
explicit sexual imagery... It is Williams's staging that does
most to justify the new title (*Vanity*). Her design consists
of three hinged frames, which are put to amazingly varied
use: wheeled around to create new locations, chess pieces,
galloping horses. For the duel Onegin spins his frame as if
playing Russian roulette, creating an unbearably prolonged
moment before it finally comes to rest and Lensky vanishes
into the dark...'
Irving Wardle, *The Times*

'Bursting through its suffocatingly formal conventions, it
explodes into ecstasies of bliss and agonies of despair... The
real strength of Richard Crane's distillation is its compelling
counterpoint between man's trivial love-games and woman's
unrequited adoration. The climax of this opposition is the
apogee of Faynia Williams's splendid direction... As Onegin
pirouettes in a frenzied mazurka, Tatyana conducts the music
like a mechanical doll, a doting creature pathetically shackled
to his insufferable vanity...'
Lindsay Paterson, *Scotsman*

# GOGOL

'He's done it again and so has she. Richard Crane's one-man show directed by Faynia Williams with her customary unearthly brilliance will be one of the great heights of this year's Festival... a performance of insight, irony, bitterness, beauty and boundless imagination with more energy and control than mortals can decently be expected to command. Gogol would be proud of his interpreters...'
Owen Dudley Edwards, *Irish Times*

'Richard Crane has devised a riveting one-man play which unites his own talents with those of the Russian writer Nikolai Gogol...'
Edinburgh *Evening News*

'The brilliant Richard Crane has demonstrated his talent at theatre festivals with what I might call a thinking man's spectaculars. Now he turns up at the Royal Court with a one-man play written and performed by himself: an equally striking exercise in drama in miniature...In Faynia Williams's fine production, he is surrounded by taxi meters ticking away his words and his life... Actor Crane's remarkable flow of words and his total identification with the morbid recluse do not conceal author Crane's gift for a phrase, or his wicked sense of fun...'
John Barber, *Daily Telegraph*

'The play depicts the plight of bureaucratic man and a vision of a world that is horrifyingly random... The play is comparable in power to Beckett and Richard Crane's performance is one of the most thoughtfully created and subtly executed that I can remember...'
*Scotsman*

# SATAN'S BALL

'The sensation of festival drama has been Richard Crane's adaptation of *The Master and Margarita*... an extraordinary and exciting assimilation of styles and influences: expressionism, morality, fairy tale, bureaucratic satire, political nightmare... directed with inventive flamboyance by Faynia Williams.. exciting in a rare theatrical way...'
Nicholas de Jongh, *Guardian*


'In the celestial cavern, complete with thunderous organ... *Satan's Ball* offers an imaginative experience of a high order... Richard Crane's adaptation and Faynia Williams's staging succeed in making the many strands intelligible in a spectacle thrilling without being hollow, blending ideas and feeling with great dramatic force. The images are by turns comic, bleak and stirring...'
J W Lambert, *Sunday Times*


'The talk of the town, the hottest ticket after *Carmen*... this spectacular production sweeps all before it, staged on great tiered platforms joined by endless flights of steps... The action encompasses a diabolical cabaret and a simpler more moving crucifixion than Oberammergau, seen appallingly high on a hill at night, through an enveloping darkness... Apart from Peter Brook, no English director has Williams's imaginative understanding of European total theatre...'
John Barber, *Daily Telegraph*


'For philosophical weight, wit and density, Richard Crane's adaptation of Bulgakov's *Master and Margarita*, was the outstanding event of the Fringe... Faynia WIlliams directs a large cast in and out of a huge constructivist set, alternating massive choral set pieces and intimate table-talk, with no sense of strain. *Satan's Ball* has everything: music, colour, choreography, excellent individual performances... Sheer circus...'
*Plays and Players*

# INTRODUCTION

You learn some thrilling and elemental truths, working with the Russians. First: that adapting novels is not enough. Hidden in these classics, there are living, sinewy dramas to be discovered and eased out into the limelight, without reference to the novels, as if they had only ever been plays. Bulgakov, Gogol, Pushkin, even Dostoyevsky*, were all theatre people, and would understand that ours is a disrespectful art and that to 'honour' the text is to kill it. I have tried in these four plays to distil the essential drama, and give it an immediate and undiluted kick, like vodka.

Secondly: that the lives of these writers are just as dramatic and sensational as the works and are inextricably woven into them. I found it was a huge help, at least in my imagination, to contain each play within the writer's extended true-life, 'to-be-or-not-to-be' moment: Dostoyevsky, led out to face the firing-squad, waiting for the command 'Fire!', then hearing across the parade-ground, a horseman galloping... Pushkin, wounded in the stomach, being carried home on the sleigh, his final moment extending unbelievably for two days... Gogol, on hunger strike and buried under a compress of hot loaves, with leeches up his nose, as 'Gogolian' doctors rushed about, failing to save him... and Bulgakov, a century later, played with by Stalin, like a gun-toting cat with a mouse, and going blind from a kidney disease, as he raced to finish *Master and Margarita*, which he knew would never be published... These writers' lives were on the edge. The battlefield in their hearts and the debating-chamber in their heads were the setting for the plays. The four characters in *Brothers Karamazov*, the three in *Vanity*, the one (split into three) in *Gogol*, are all contrasting portraits of the writers. In *Satan's Ball*, the whole story of the devil coming to Moscow, within which a student (Bezdomny) is writing a play about Christ, within which a disciple (Matthew) is spinning a myth for future generations, the whole matrioshka-like story, in my play, is the creation of The Master, alias Bulgakov; that's why he is blind.

---

*Dostoyevsky survived his time in Omsk Prison by directing pantomimes and vaudevilles with his fellow inmates.

Thirdly: that artists, writers and composers who inspired or were inspired by the Russian writers, are there waiting to be used. The seed of Karamazov sprang from Dostoyevsky's reading of Schiller; so, looking for lyrics for the songs, I adapted Schiller odes, ending with the irrepressible *Ode to Joy*. *Vanity*, distancing itself from Tchaikovsky, recalls the haunting intimacy of Prokofiev's *Eugene Onegin*, the missing sections of which, just a year before our premiere, had been rediscovered and performed by Edward Downes. In *Gogol*, there is a snatch of a song by Benjamin Britten, about old Abram Brown and his long brown coat. *Satan's Ball* ends with Alexander Blok's *The Twelve*, his stern and pitiless hymn to the future. Dreaming up a set for that show, we were inspired by the Tower, designed but never built, by the Constructivist Vladimir Tatlin, celebrating the Collective Power of Man.

Which brings me to 'fourthly'.

The team is all. These are multi-artform co-creations and they begin with the bond between writer and director.

## SATAN'S BALL

All these plays were set in motion by Faynia Williams. Russian was her subject and she unlocked for me a bottomless treasure-chest of ideas. Director/designer, translator, 'fiercest critic' and life companion, she was an essential co-creator at every stage of the plays. She had succeeded me as Bradford University's Fellow in Theatre, a unique non-academic post which with Chris Parr before us and Graham Devlin and Ruth Mackenzie following, made Bradford 'the finest student theatre in the country'\*, winning international acclaim and many awards. We regularly took companies of sixty or more to the Edinburgh Festival, including engineers and mountaineers. *Satan's Ball* was to be Faynia's final Edinburgh with Bradford, fulfilling a dream begun with the Russianist Michael Glenny, to put Bulgakov's masterpiece on the stage.

We sat for a day in the Old Chaplaincy (now Bedlam Theatre), with its forty-foot high gothic vaulting and organ pipes, envisaging the floor raised to gallery level, creating a 'rink effect' out of which Tatlin's Tower, erected by Bradford's engineers and mountaineers,

\*Arts Council Review

would spiral up into the roof. The three Suprematist levels, the square, the circle, and the triangle, would represent Moscow, Jerusalem and 'limbo'. The whole would be the Tower of State, with red-robed heroes poised biomechanically and singing in unison; then it would become Golgotha, with Yeshua crucified naked against the organ-pipes, as they roared out the Matthew Passion; and at the climax, the Tower would explode into the venue for the Ball, with lobotomized guests streaming out from its base, to the music of Woland and his hellish band.

## GOGOL

We moved to Brighton after *Satan's Ball*, into a house that was previously multiple bedsits. In each room, there was a black, round-edged, metal electricity meter with little clock-faces and dials. Strung up on fishing wire, like giant leeches, these became the scenographic starting-point for *Gogol*. Without the financial guarantee of a university, we were going minimalist all the way. 'O' was the key, the design concept and the budget: an invisible solo (so middling you wouldn't notice him), in a loop, on a roundabout. Gogol – 'There are four 'O's in my name' – was the literary parent of Bulgakov and all paths out of *Satan's Ball* led to him; but the main route was a book: Nabokov's monograph *Nikolai Gogol*. Not a biography, not lit crit, this incendiary intertwining of two writers' passions, carries you along breathless on an icy whirlwind. You can't *not* want to write a play, with this wealth of crazy detail, siphoned into the overcoat of the invisible clerk. *Dead Souls, The Government Inspector, The Coat, The Nose, Nevsky Prospekt* and *Diary of a Madman*, all these I boiled down to their essence and out came the present-day Final Demands Clerk in the London Electricity Board.

## VANITY

As the set was the key to *Satan's Ball*, and the props were the key to *Gogol*, so it was the music and the musicality of the verse, that unlocked the dramatizing of *Eugene Onegin*, setting it free from grand opera and restoring it to a chamber work. I used Pushkin's complex and delightful stanza form, as the basis for telling the story. The pattern of the seasons, the pace of social occasions trip along to the trochaic equivalent of a dance. But then it slips a gear, first into dramatic iambics, when we hear the dreams and fears that are surging behind the mask; then dangerously into prose, as characters transgress and lose their way. Sanity and society are kept on the rails by strictly choreographed verse. Madness and rebellion have harsher unknown rhythms. The abyss is never far away.

We decided early on that this was a three-hander, each character contained in his or her own fragile world, and able to manoeuvre in and out of one another's domain. This mobility translated into three pieces of furniture, or 'furnits', designed like a vanity mirror with a blank frame, a drawer for storing props, and casters to run on. Placed together and angled these could make a bay window with a window seat, or a row of mirrors in a ballroom. Separated, they could be giant chess pieces, horses, a drinks trolley, a dressing-table, a bench by the lake, and instruments of death in the duelling scene. Olga, partnering Onegin at the ball, was a flying red ribbon, snatched from the props drawer and whirled around Korean dancer-style and cracked like a whip.

## BROTHERS KARAMAZOV

John Drummond, Director of the Edinburgh International Festival and the Diaghilev of his day, was looking for rough brilliance, to be lifted from the jungle of the Fringe and transplanted into the orderly garden of the main programme. He had seen *Vanity* and *Gogol* and rang up one day with the offer of a commission: perhaps something on Dostoyevsky who that year would be celebrating a double anniversary – 150 years since his birth, 100 since his death. We went away to have a think. The only Dostoyevsky I had read, had been *Crime and Punishment,* already much dramatized. Faynia suggested *Karamazov* – it's not as monumental as you think: a murder mystery, family comedy, tangled love story, courtroom drama, spiced with epilepsy and theology – but we would have to work fast. It was already February and publicity had to be got out. Brighton Theatre was to be the first Fringe company ever to appear on the Edinburgh main programme and we would need to secure a top-quality cast. There was a national tour to be arranged, and the possibility, if we could break the Thatcher ban on cultural links with Moscow, of a Soviet Union tour.

We were so busy setting it all up and so successful with the publicity, that the box office had opened and every ticket had been sold, before a word of the play was written. We had cast eight, high-quality actors – four male, four female – and I was going to write the play around them; but the more I got into the story, the more the nightmare truth began to dawn: this play was a four-hander. Dostoyevsky, in a letter, says the story of the Karamazovs can be seen from four view-points, through the eyes of each of the brothers: Dmitry, the romantic; Ivan the intellectual; Alyosha, the spiritual, and Smerdyakov, the physical. It was a male quartet. The four actresses had to go.

With the casting decision made, the writing came quickly. It was completed in Wimbledon fortnight, the script landing hot off the typewriter, on the first day of rehearsal. It was a play of conversation and debate; of forensic argument, and 'talking stupidly'; also journeying down a long road, and tumbling from the height of the Madonna to the depth of Sodom; of the depraved father being killed and the saintly father dying; of singing and dancing, of loving and murdering; of the corn of wheat rotting in the earth to produce new life.

The set was a table, surreally extended with arms and a diagonal foot-piece, like a Russian Orthodox cross, and then sloped and perspectivized, to make couches for reclining on, a raked floor for dancing and the long downhill road. Songs were *a capella* in four-part harmony, with music by Stephen Boxer who was to play Alyosha. The theatre in Edinburgh was the panelled basement of the Freemasons' Hall with the audience crowded in on three sides. Sensuality was evoked by a bear-like fur coat, which each brother would be robed in and would grow into at the point in the play when he was closest to his depraved father. Spirituality was evoked by a flowing monk's cloak which each brother would adopt, to play Zosima, the Grand Inquisitor and the Devil.

The astonishing (fifth) truth of the Russian plays, is that once they are up and running, they grow lives of their own. They travel the world, rooting themselves in whatever soil they land in – a gas works in Sweden, a psychiatric hospital in Poland, a fortified convent in Belfast, a schoolroom in Adelaide, a bank in New York, a ballroom in Moscow – even when, as in the Russian tour, we were delivering back to them, their own classic. Theatre was at that time the only dialogue, and by candle-light in Georgia (there were power cuts), we thawed out a small portion of the cultural freeze, exchanging with the Rustaveli Theatre, our Dostoyevsky for their Shakespeare. Then in the National Theatre of Romania in 1991, just a year after the execution of their own depraved father-figure, the play with its rich absurd humour and its hymn to a new liberated 'fatherless' state, was suddenly Romanian to the core.

These plays are on a journey and it's your pleasure now to travel with them, whether it's Onegin 'free to go', circling the world and coming back to where he started; or Pilate and Yeshua walking on and debating along the endless path of light; or Ivan Karamazov's furious atheist on the quadrillion kilometre road; or Dmitry's dream hero in his tumbril, heading for the guillotine and taking a detour via Africa; or Gogol's anonymous clerk in his troika, racing and singing, the wind in his hair, a great Nose in a Coat, in the extended pre-crash, present moment for ever.

*Richard Crane, Brighton 2011*

# BROTHERS KARAMAZOV

## AFTER DOSTOYEVSKY

Peter Kelly, Bruce Alexander, Will Knightley and Stephen Boxer in the
West End production (illustration from *Punch*)

# Characters

DMITRY

– also plays KARAMAZOV, DEVIL

IVAN

– also plays KARAMAZOV, KATERINA,
GRAND INQUISITOR

ALYOSHA

– also plays ZOSIMA, KARAMAZOV,
DEFENCE COUNSEL

SMERDYAKOV

– also plays KARAMAZOV, GRUSHENKA,
ZOSIMA, PROSECUTION COUNSEL

Each brother is essentially himself throughout the
play, and assumes other roles as an extension of his
character. All, in turn, play their father Karamazov,
simply by donning a massive, animal-like fur coat.
Similarly, the spiritual parent – Zosima, the Grand
Inquisitor, the Devil – is achieved by donning a vast,
flowing monk's cloak. No change other than a softening
of voice and gesture is required for the playing of
Katerina and Grushenka.

*Brothers Karamazov* was first performed by Brighton Theatre, at the Edinburgh International Festival 19th August 1981, with the following cast:

DMITRY, Bruce Alexander
IVAN, Alan Rickman
ALYOSHA, Stephen Boxer
SMERDYAKOV, Peter Kelly

*Directed and designed by* Faynia Williams
*Music by* Stephen Boxer

The production toured Russia, Georgia and the UK, and opened at the Fortune Theatre London, 7th November 1981, with the following cast:

DMITRY, Bruce Alexander
IVAN, Will Knightley
ALYOSHA, Stephen Boxer
SMERDYAKOV, Peter Kelly

*Directed and designed by* Faynia Williams

*Brothers Karamazov* was nominated Best Director (Faynia Williams), Best Actor (Alan Rickman), Best Supporting Actor (Peter Kelly) in the Plays and Players Awards 1981.

Music by Stephen Boxer is obtainable from Gardner Herrity Ltd, 24 Conway St, London W1T 6BG, info@gardnerherrity.co.uk

# ACT ONE

## THE HEART OF MAN

BROTHERS: *(Sing.)*
>Over barren blackened earth
>Mother Ceres angry seeks
>signs of mortal man's true worth
>but every blackened meadow reeks.

>Foul the sky and vile the land
>ploughshares beaten into guns;
>brother dead by brother's hand
>father murdered by his sons.

>Hope in stench of corpses lies,
>blood and tears soak the plain.
>Mother Ceres angry cries:
>Live my child live again!
>Live my child live again!

*Monastery clock strikes twelve. DMITRY robes SMERDYAKOV in the fur coat as KARAMAZOV. IVAN robes ALYOSHA in the hooded cloak as ZOSIMA.*

*KARAMAZOV and IVAN before ZOSIMA. ZOSIMA bows low. KARAMAZOV responds likewise.*

ZOSIMA: Fyodor Pavlovich Karamazov.

KARAMAZOV: Most esteemed and holy elder ZOSIMA. We're deeply grateful to your reverence for agreeing to settle our little dispute.

ZOSIMA: Are all your sons here?

KARAMAZOV: All except the oldest, Dmitry, sainted father.

ZOSIMA: Is he coming?

KARAMAZOV: I should hope so. He's the cause of it: the little hiccup in our relationship which your eminence is going to sort out.

ZOSIMA: Please make yourselves comfortable. *(Sits.)*

KARAMAZOV: Very gracious of you blessed father, and may I say how simple and humbling your little cell is, with its gnarled bench and scrubbed floor, and how extremely touched we are that your reverence is giving up his precious time, not to say his last moments, if what rumour says is true –

ZOSIMA: Thank you for your concern.

KARAMAZOV: It's not true is it blessed father? You look so happy.

ZOSIMA: Where I am going is a happy place.

KARAMAZOV: Well it would be wouldn't it? You're a saint divine father and good luck to you, and I'm sure I speak for all the millions of lesser mortals who could never hope to achieve such a spiritual altitude your eminence. We're worms, mere worms, who wriggle with doubt at the thought of dying and nothing hereafter but "burdock to grace our graves", as the poet so aptly put it.

ZOSIMA: Don't be ashamed of having doubts. Be yourself.

KARAMAZOV: That's a risk I'd rather not take, blessed father. I'm worthless and depraved and I play the fool and never stop talking, to cover myself, so people will like me. As it says in the Gospel: "In the beginning was the Word" – and do you know why? Because God couldn't stand the silence! Drove him so mad, he made the world! *(Pause.)* Unnatural, silence. Can't stand it. No one can – except Ivan. He's like a gravestone. Stands there for hours ticking over like a clock. What's he thinking about? Have a guess holy elder. He's a riddle to me. *(Grins at IVAN.)*

IVAN: *(Thinks aloud.)* I hate my father. I hate his fat little face and the fleshy bags under his eyes. I hate his stumps of black teeth rotting behind his flabby lips and the wash of saliva when he speaks, and his adam's apple bobbing against his chin like a purse…

ZOSIMA: *(To KARAMAZOV.)* What are you afraid of?

KARAMAZOV: Nothing! And that's the awful thing your reverence. Nothing – that great pit. The yawning void. The awful eternity of nothing. That's what I'm afraid of.

ZOSIMA: Is that why you build defences?

KARAMAZOV: You mean money? Yes it is. And don't say it's evil. It's not evil at all. It's the *root* of all evil, and I've spent my life blessed elder, digging up those roots and selling them. When I started out, I didn't have two beans to rub together. Now I'm worth 100,000, and a darn sight more if I wasn't so generous.

ZOSIMA: We're very grateful for your donation.

KARAMAZOV: Have you invested it? You ought to. Our blessed Lord and Saviour was a capitalist. Parable of the Talents. "For unto everyone that hath, shall be given, but from him that hath not, shall be taken away, even that which he hath."

ZOSIMA: What did he mean by that?

KARAMAZOV: I haven't a clue divine father. I'm a fool, a born joker! I've lost two wives, did you know that? Lovely creatures, your holiness. I'd have gone under if I couldn't laugh.

ZOSIMA: You're not laughing.

KARAMAZOV: Oh I am! All the time! And the worst of it is, I always know when my jokes are falling flat. I feel my cheeks begin to stick to my gums, like a spasm. But I keep going. I'm an idiot, a saintly fool, holy elder. But at least I'm honest about it, which proves it because all fools are honest.

ZOSIMA: You're not a fool.

KARAMAZOV: What am I then? Tell me. If you can show me there's more to life than cabbage soup, I'll kiss your feet and bless the womb that bore you, and the paps that you sucked, the blessed paps! – I'm a sensualist holy father. So you tell me. What must I do to inherit eternal life?

ZOSIMA: You know what you must do.

KARAMAZOV: Live on gudgeons? Deny God's work and buy my way out of it with dry bread and gudgeons?

ZOSIMA: Drink less, talk less, close your brothels and public houses.

KARAMAZOV: Now wait a minute –

ZOSIMA: Or just two or three of them.

KARAMAZOV: My establishments are founded on the precepts of our blessed Lord Jesus Christ, who wasn't averse to turning water into wine and having himself rubbed over by a prostitute. Or has your rarified eminence forgotten that?

ZOSIMA: Above all, do not tell lies.

KARAMAZOV: It's true! It's in the Bible!

ZOSIMA: Especially to yourself. The man who lies and listens to his lies, ceases to respect himself and those around him.

KARAMAZOV: All right I'm a liar, and that's the truth, so I'm not a liar.

ZOSIMA: Such a man finds it easy and pleasant to take offence.

KARAMAZOV: Who's taking offence?

ZOSIMA: Run from lies!

KARAMAZOV: You're the liar! You're a *fake*! I owe nothing to you holy quack. You stole my Alyosha, my youngest boy. He'd just come back to me of his own free will. I'd waited twenty years. Can't stand children. Innocence depresses me. He'd come back a man, with fire in his loins. I could have shown him the world! All this shall be yours, if you'll only *enjoy* it! But you nipped him in the bud didn't you? No use to me now is he? All he can do now is hoodwink me into coming to see you, when I should be in court! Dmitry should be dragged howling down the mines! But

24

you'll probably let him off with a wink, won't you gelded elder? And talking of courts, what do you think of our judicial system? Should the church have the right to try social matters, or should it keep its nose clean? I'm trying to bring the gravestone into the conversation. He wrote an article on it.

ZOSIMA: I've heard about it.

KARAMAZOV: Clever isn't he? Mathematical nihilist. Strings words together and strangles you with them. *(To IVAN.)* Would you care to respond Ivan? He's dying. He needs comfort. Tell him how the pearly gates will be slammed in his face!

IVAN: My contention was that though church and state will of course go on for ever, they will always be separate, because the basis of any compromise between them, is inherently false. Originally, the church was independent, owing allegiance only to God, but when it became contained within the Roman state, it necessarily lost its edge, having to cooperate with Caesar. I maintained therefore, that for the church to be true to the rock on which it stands, it must overtake Caesar and *replace* the state, so that all decisions, judgments and policies, are directed towards one absolute truth. Under the present separation, it is possible, for instance, for a criminal to be sentenced by the state, but remain morally innocent. When the church becomes the state – which should be the avowed aim of Christian society – there will be no such refuge. The criminal will have offended against Christ himself, thus losing all hope of eternal life.

ZOSIMA: Would you welcome this absolute power for the church?

IVAN: I'm simply an observer.

ZOSIMA: But you have opinions.

IVAN: I have observed that civilization is based on the lie of immortality.

ZOSIMA: Where does that lead you?

IVAN: It leads me to observe that if this lie were exposed, the moral order would dry up, and everything would be permitted, even cannibalism and parricide.

KARAMAZOV: Aha! The excuse! Note that holy elder. When they kill me, remember, he's got permission in writing!

*DMITRY bursts in.*

DMITRY: Smerdyakov told me one o'clock. You've been waiting. I apologize. *(Kneels before ZOSIMA.)* Bless me holy father for I have sinned.

KARAMAZOV: Right! To business!

DMITRY: Wait a minute.

KARAMAZOV: We've waited an hour!

ZOSIMA: *(Blesses DMITRY.)* You are welcome here. We were discussing a theory of your brother's, which I should like to take further. He was saying that for the unbeliever, everything is permitted, even criminal behaviour. If this were so, then surely crime should not only be permitted, but seen as necessary.

DMITRY: Crime necessary?
*(Looks at KARAMAZOV.)* I'll remember that.

IVAN: I said without immortality, there can be no virtue.

KARAMAZOV: May we proceed holy judge?

ZOSIMA: But you don't altogether reject immortality?

KARAMAZOV: *I* do.

IVAN: *(Smiles.)*

KARAMAZOV: I reject it for wasting valuable time. We are here to judge this prodigal son, who took his inheritance and a great deal more, and squandered it, and then returned to his loving father, demanding prime cuts off the fatted calf.

DMITRY: Holy father, he threw me out when I was three years old and ever since, he's been chalking up my debts and deducting them from the money left to *me* by my mother.

KARAMAZOV: A tiny proportion of your mother's estate was set aside for your education. This, in my kindness, I spent twice over.

DMITRY: You owe me 28,000. He extorted it from my mother.

KARAMAZOV: It was legally mine. She was my wife.

DMITRY: He used to beat her. He threw her out. She starved to death.

KARAMAZOV: She used to beat *me*. She ran off with a student. And she died of typhus.

DMITRY: I'm not asking holy elder, for her whole estate –

KARAMAZOV: You're not asking for any of it! I have documents to prove that when I gave you the last 6000, you renounced all further claims. All monies thereafter, were loans to be repaid. You gave me promissory notes for all these loans –

DMITRY: Which he passed on to a third party, to sue me and have me put away.

KARAMAZOV: I don't deny that, and I don't deny, dreadful judge, that he then set about seducing the third party, a lady of impeccable virtue –

DMITRY: She's a slut and I love her.

KARAMAZOV: Mitya my boy, you're engaged –

DMITRY: I love Grushenka.

KARAMAZOV: He's engaged to Katerina Ivanovna Verkhovsteva.

DMITRY: And Grushenka loves me.

KARAMAZOV: She doesn't. She loves me.

DMITRY: She loathes you.

KARAMAZOV: She adores me.

DMITRY: He's trying to buy her from me. He has 3000 roubles in an envelope waiting –

KARAMAZOV: *(White with anger.)* Who told you that?

DMITRY: It's under your pillow with a note.

KARAMAZOV: And she'll come for it.

DMITRY: She'll die first.

KARAMAZOV: He's threatening to kill her!

DMITRY: I love her! She's mine!!

KARAMAZOV: She needs my protection.

DMITRY: How can such a man live!

KARAMAZOV: Listen to the parricide!

DMITRY: How can he pollute the earth with his life!

KARAMAZOV: He's afraid if I marry Grushenka, he'll lose his inheritance. They all are. They're not sons. They're vultures!

ZOSIMA: *(Rises.)*

DMITRY: *(Weeping.)* I came here holy father, in good faith, to hold out my hands and embrace him like a son –

KARAMAZOV: If you have any honour in your shrivelling flesh, holy worm, you will drag his claws from my neck and judge him! Judge him!

*ZOSIMA falls at DMITRY's feet and bows to the ground. DMITRY moves away quickly.*

*ALYOSHA throws back the cloak.*

ALYOSHA: *(Kneeling.)* There was a mad girl, about twenty, under five foot, healthy, red face, slack mouth, fixed vacant eyes. Thick mass of black hair, always matted with mud and splinters and bits of straw. Slept in gardens and barns. Walked round and round in and out of houses. People gave her food which she gave to stray dogs, and clothing and money which she left neatly in the church porch. She lived on water and black bread. No one teased her or touched her. She was holy.

A group of overgrown boys had drunk too much. It was a hot cloudy night. They sang songs and staggered down

the lane by the kitchen gardens. The loudest and oldest
had a fat little face, and fleshy bags under his eyes. They
saw the mad girl fast asleep in the nettles. Could this
animal possibly be a woman? His adam's apple bobbed.
Spit washed from his lips. Only one way to find out! They
stood around laughing and egged him on. She woke up.
He gagged her, held her down. The storm burst.

She walked round and round, in and out of houses. The
child inside her kicked and turned over. People gave her
food, wanted to help her. She ran out into the teeming
night, down the sodden lane, by the kitchen gardens;
tore herself scrambling over the fence; broke the window
into the bath-house; fell on the stone floor, writhing and
groaning, pouring blood, splitting, shrieking, dying – as the
child was born!

*Extended musical cry splits into three parts over the last lines of
the speech. SMERDYAKOV slowly slithers from the coat as from an
outer skin.*

*IVAN, SMERDYAKOV.*

SMERDYAKOV: You know sir, I've been thinking. If the
rumours are true –

IVAN: What rumours Smerdyakov?

SMERDYAKOV: That you're my brother. It makes sense.
Explains our understanding, how I always seem to know
what you're thinking sir. I was trying to put it down to
clairvoyance, possible related to my epilepsy, but it's much
simpler than that sir. It's genetic – substantiated also by us
having spent our infancy in the same environment.

IVAN: This doesn't put us on an equal footing Smerdyakov.

SMERDYAKOV: Oh God forbid sir, if he exists. I wouldn't
presume to equate myself with such a clever man as you
sir! Do you remember when you left sir, walked out on me
at the age of six? I was so distressed when you closed the
door, I sat there looking at it for half an hour. They called
me contemplative, because I can do that: sit still for hours
on end and not move a hair. Then I got up and opened the

door, put my finger in the crack and slammed it shut and held it for ten seconds.

*Pause.*

*DMITRY calls from the shadows.*

DMITRY: Alyosha! Quick! Down here!

ALYOSHA: Mitya!

DMITRY: Ssh little brother!

ALYOSHA: *(Whispers.)* Why are you whispering?

DMITRY: Secret. I've been waiting for you. I knew you'd come. I want to tell you everything. *(Hugs him.)* I love you little monk. I actually in all the world, love no one but you. And that slut Grushenka – I hate her!

ALYOSHA: Mitya listen –

DMITRY: *(Sings.)* Glory to God in the highest!
Glory to God in *me*!

ALYOSHA: *(Weeping.)* The elder bowed down to you and kissed the earth. That means you will suffer.

DMITRY: Let me look at you. Don't cry. You have a hold on life Alyosha. Only you can give me strength. Tomorrow my life is ending and beginning. I shall fly to the clouds, then dive down the chasm. *(He lies back.)* Do you know what that's like? Nor do I. That's why I love it. Look at the sky. Bright blue. And the leaves. It's still summer.

*(Sings.)* Joy divine adored immortal
daughter of Elysium…
Can't remember the words – *(Bursts into tears.)*

*Pause.*

ALYOSHA: Come with me to see father.

DMITRY: *(Sings softly as Alyosha continues.)*
Over barren blackened earth…

ALYOSHA: He wants to love you. He wants you to love him. But he's afraid…

DMITRY: *(Continuing.)* ...Mother Ceres angry seeks
  signs of mortal man's true worth...

  Depressing isn't it? But it can't depress us: we're
  Karamazovs! We leap down the pit and the fall is beautiful.
  Why try to make sense of it? It's all riddles and mysteries.
  Ivan thinks he can unravel them, but turn his back, and
  they're at each other, seething like snakes. Beauty is a
  terrible thing little brother: a furnace! Soars to the highest
  and purest Madonna, then plunges to Sodom, the lowest
  pit. And man contains it all. Can't understand why his
  head is ashamed and his body roars! He tries to stifle it
  with science, but as long as he lives, the fight goes on: God
  and the devil raging like bulls, and the battlefield is the
  heart of man!

  *Ivan, Smerdyakov.*

SMERDYAKOV: Everything makes sense doesn't it sir? God
  was invented to keep ignorant folk in order with fairy-
  tales about two and two making five. Intelligent folk can
  see through the lie. We can do as we like. Everything is
  permitted – except if you're epileptic. What happens sir, if
  an intelligent man has something inside he can't control?

IVAN: He hangs himself Smerdyakov.

SMERDYAKOV: Oh. Does he? *(Pause.)* Why did you come
  home sir? All you've done is prowl about this tomb of
  a house, like a caged animal. You're a free man. You're
  lucky. You can do as you like. Is it Miss Katerina sir? Mr
  Dmitry's finacee? You've taken a shine to her haven't you?
  I can tell. And if you want my advice sir, you ought to try
  a bit harder. Drag her screaming to the altar. She'd like
  that. And you'd get satisfaction from it as well, if you ask
  me sir... *(Pause.)* It's turned chilly. Put this on *(The fur coat).*
  You'll catch cold.

  *He helps IVAN/KARAMAZOV into the coat.*

  There's a worm in you, isn't there sir? Like in all the
  Karamazovs. And it needs feeding. I know sir. There's a
  tiny worm in me...

*Alyosha, Dmitry.*

ALYOSHA: What do you want me to do?

DMITRY: Go to Katerina. Tell her it's over, finished.

ALYOSHA: Don't you think you should do that?

DMITRY: I owe her money – 3000! I spent it on Grushenka.

ALYOSHA: All of it?

DMITRY: Half of it.

ALYOSHA: Give her the other half.

DMITRY: I don't have it.

ALYOSHA: Where is it?

DMITRY: I spent it.

ALYOSHA: *(Laughs.)* You're mad!

DMITRY: I'm lying little brother. I can tell you because I love you. It's here. *(Beats his breast.)* My salvation. I'm not a thief! I'm not a thief! *(Pause.)* I saw the Madonna on the streets of Sodom, and bought her outright. Grushenka, she's a witch! You can feel it in every curve of her body, in the smallest toe of her tiny foot, which I dared to kiss, and that's all I did, and it's costing me 3000. You must get it for me.

ALYOSHA: Where from?

KARAMAZOV/IVAN: *(To SMERDYAKOV.)* Tell her to come. She must come.

DMITRY: Go to father. He's got it.

KARAMAZOV: Tell her what I've got for her.

DMITRY: 3000 roubles in an envelope. Smerdyakov told me.

KARAMAZOV: Tell her to come to me by night. I'll be waiting. Watch out for her.

DMITRY: He'll give it to her if she comes. That's why I'm here, watching out for her.

KARAMAZOV: Don't let anyone else in.

ALYOSHA: But how will you stop them?

DMITRY: I won't need to, if you ask him –

ALYOSHA: But what if he won't give it to me?

DMITRY: Then I'll kill him! I'll beat his head in!

*KARAMAZOV is seated, slightly drunk, after dinner. SMERDYAKOV attends.*

KARAMAZOV: Alyosha! Come on in boy!

ALYOSHA: *(Approaches.)*

KARAMAZOV: You look starved. Aren't they feeding you? You've just missed Smerdyakov's *piece de resistance*! Fish soup. Is there any left?

ALYOSHA: I've eaten already.

KARAMAZOV: Have some coffee and cognac. You look sober.

ALYOSHA: No thanks.

KARAMAZOV: And cherry jam. Have we got some cherry jam?

ALYOSHA: I'm really not hungry father.

KARAMAZOV: What do you want then? Money?

ALYOSHA: 3000.

KARAMAZOV: You shall have it! But first you must sing for it. We want your opinion. Balaam's ass here has been talking his broth-brewer's head off and I didn't even have to flog him! What do you want 3000 for?

ALYOSHA: I'm leaving the monastery. Father ZOSIMA says I should live in the world.

KARAMAZOV: I told you he was a sensualist didn't I? He has women. They queue up for him every night. And they pay him for it –

ALYOSHA: But I've decided not to leave the monastery while he lives.

KARAMAZOV: He didn't fool me, sitting there like a stuffed owl. He's a jackdaw. Can't trust him an inch. Unlike

Smerdyakov here who is a paragon of obedience and servility. He used to hang cats. Did you know that? Vicious brute. He'd get a cat and stroke it, get it purring, playing with a piece of string, then he's slip the string round its neck and hang it up. Then he'd dress himself in a sheet, sing a requiem, lay it out, sprinkling it with scented water, then cradle it like a dead child and bury it, tears streaming down his face. I caught him at it once, gave him such a walloping he had a fit. Little sadist! Blasphemy! What would the neighbours say? It was their cat! What were we talking about?

SMERDYAKOV: We were talking about the soldier who was taken prisoner by the Turks.

KARAMAZOV: Tell him about it. I want his opinion.

SMERDYAKOV: Well sir, they told him to spit on the cross, and he wouldn't do it, so they flayed him alive. And now everyone's crowing about it as if he'd done something good.

KARAMAZOV: And so he has. He should be canonized. Send his skin to the monastery. Think of the crowds. We'd make a mint!

ALYOSHA: What are you saying Smerdyakov?

SMERDYAKOV: Well sir, look at it this way. I'm a prisoner. They're going to skin me if I don't spit. So I spit. Why not? I want to stay alive.

ALYOSHA: You'd be cursed by God.

KARAMAZOV: You tell him boy, tell him!

SMERDYAKOV: What does that mean sir?

ALYOSHA: You'd be excluded from the faith.

SMERDYAKOV: Fair enough. So I'm a heathen. They don't mind. They get by. And I can always come back, can't I sir, if I repent my action – on account of the infinite mercy of God. To keep your faith when you don't have to, and lose your skin for it, strikes me sir, as an act of pure pig-headed swank. I wouldn't do it.

ALYOSHA: A strong faith cannot be renounced.

SMERDYAKOV: But that's just it sir! My faith *isn't* strong. It's frail as a leaf. Strong faith is telling mountains to go jump in the sea. I couldn't even say that to a mole-hill! I'm weak and wavery, like the vast majority of Christian souls. Only difference is, I'm honest about it.

KARAMAZOV: What shall we do with him Alyosha? Whip him or sell him to the Jesuits?

SMERDYAKOV: You can make fun of me if you like sir. I'm only a lackey.

ALYOSHA: You've been talking to Ivan.

SMERDYAKOV: He's a clever man sir.

ALYOSHA: He's unhappy.

SMERDYAKOV: *(Angry.)* Perhaps he should be the judge of that sir. That's what gets me about the church. They tell you what to feel – don't let you work it out for yourself. And I'll tell you why they do that: because they know it's a sham. There's no logic in it. It's all high-falluting waffle, invented by the ruling classes, to keep the working man in his place!

KARAMAZOV: *(Applauds.)* Well said boy! I like him. Makes me laugh. Remind me to give you a bonus. You know what he said the other day? He'd been reading his Bible. He's a clever crawler you must admit. He said, if God made the world, beginning with day and night, then the firmament on the second day, herbs and fruit on the day after, but waited till the fourth day to make the sun, moon and stars, where in heaven or hell did he think he got the light from on the first day! *(Laughs.)* My cheeks are sticking to my gums. I can feel it like a spasm. *(To ALYOSHA.)* Have some brandy. Come on! Tell me once and for all: Is there a God?

ALYOSHA: Yes there is.

KARAMAZOV: And immortality?

ALYOSHA: Yes there is.

KARAMAZOV: And brandy? Can you get brandy up there? What happens when you die? Do they come for you with hooks? What do they attach them to? The ceiling? Where is it written that hell has a ceiling? You show me the ceiling, I'll believe in the hooks. Until then it's a fake. I won't touch it.

*ALYOSHA giggles. This grows through KARAMAZOV's speech into a harsh laugh, then a shrieking fit.*

What's funny? You're like your mother. She used to giggle like that. I used to come in and surprise her; crawl up to her and tickle her feet. And always that sharp little laugh, like a bell. I loved it. Every time. And it got louder as I hugged her, warning me: Go away! *(Hugs ALYOSHA.)* Made me mad as I gripped her. It jangled and clanged as she swung from side to side. I loved her! I loved her! My Madonna of the Bells! I'd give anything, anything – 3000, 20,000! – to hug her and hear the bells!

*ALYOSHA is shrieking. DMITRY bursts in.*

DMITRY: Grushenka! Where is she? She's here! I saw her! Turning off towards the house. Where is she?

SMERDYAKOV: *(Running to him.)* Mr Dmitry!

DMITRY: *(Seizing him.)* You didn't tell me!

SMERDYAKOV: She isn't here!

DMITRY: I saw her! *(Throws him down.)*

SMERDYAKOV: You can't have seen her!

*DMITRY drags KARAMAZOV from ALYOSHA. KARAMAZOV is limp like a dead beast in the coat.*

DMITRY: Where is she? Where's the money? You gave her the money!

SMERDYAKOV: *(Trying to restrain him.)* She can't have got in sir! The back door's locked!

*DMITRY throws KARAMAZOV down. He tries to rise, is kicked in the face.*

DMITRY: I'll kill you for this! I'll kill you! I'll kill you! I'll kill you – !

SMERDYAKOV: No sir! No sir! Stop! Stop!

*DMITRY falls on KARAMAZOV, tearing at the coat.*

DMITRY: You stole her! She's mine! Grushenka's mine!

SMERDYAKOV: Help! Help! He's killing him! He's killing him!

DMITRY: *(Stripping the coat from him like skinning a bear.)* She's mine! She's mine! Grushenka's mine! She's mine… *(Hugging the coat and sobbing.)* She's mine… my Grushenka… my Grushenka… mine…mine…

*Pause.*

SMERDYAKOV: *(Sings.)*
Love I love you
I'll love you always
but I am leaving
don't weep for me.

Oh Lord listen
and bless my darling
for none is lovely as she –
none is lovely as she.

Love I love you
I'll love you always
but I am leaving
don't weep for me.

Oh Lord listen
and bless my darling
for none is lovely as she –
none is lovely as she.

*Repeats song softly through the next scene.*

ALYOSHA: *(As if in a dream.)* Katerina Ivanovna, I've come to you with a message from my brother. He asked me to say good-bye. I know it's a shock for you. You must be so unhappy…

KATERINA/IVAN: *(Reclining.)* I was expecting it.

ALYOSHA: He needs help. He nearly killed my father tonight.

KATERINA: Did he mention the sum of 3000 roubles?

ALYOSHA: He said you must have it back. He's not a thief.

KATERINA: You must tell him not to be ashamed. I want him to keep it.

ALYOSHA: He doesn't love you.

KATERINA: Whom does he love?

ALYOSHA: Grushenka. He wants to marry her.

KATERINA: *(Smiles.)* She won't have him.

ALYOSHA: Then he'll kill himself.

KATERINA: You must tell him I'm here, and all I want to do is comfort him. I will love him quietly all my life. Whenever he needs me, I am here.

ALYOSHA: What about Grushenka?

KATERINA: She's here too. *(To GRUSHENKA.)* You can come in now my angel.

*SMERDYAKOV stops singing.*

GRUSHENKA/SMERDYAKOV: *(Reclines.)* Katerina asked me to be here.

KATERINA: And she came to me. She's lovely.

GRUSHENKA: We never met before this evening.

KATERINA: But we feel we've known each other always.

ALYOSHA: I thought you were deadly rivals.

GRUSHENKA: *(Laughs.)* That shows how young you are.

KATERINA: And how little you understand women.

GRUSHENKA: I've told Katerina everything.

KATERINA: She's a darling. I want to kiss her.

GRUSHENKA: You're so sweet to me dear lady.

KATERINA: She's had such a wretched life.

GRUSHENKA: I don't deserve your kindness.

KATERINA: She was hopelessly in love with an officer, five years ago.

GRUSHENKA: But he was engaged to another. We had to part.

KATERINA: Now his wife is dead, and he has written to Grushenka that he is free at last and coming back to her.

GRUSHENKA: So romantic isn't it? And so convenient.

KATERINA: She's overjoyed. The only man she ever loved!

GRUSHENKA: You're so obliging sweet lady, to have helped me make up my mind.

KATERINA: It was made up already, and I'm so happy for you. I want to kiss your hand a hundred times.

GRUSHENKA: *(Laughs.)* You'll make me ashamed dear lady, kissing me in front of this young man!

KATERINA: You could never be ashamed.

GRUSHENKA: You don't know me. I'm wicked.

KATERINA: You're an angel, and you're saving my Dmitry.

GRUSHENKA: We had such fun together. For just one hour. He was a darling.

KATERINA: But that's over and you're going to tell him how your true love has returned, and you're hoping to be married.

GRUSHENKA: You make it sound so simple.

KATERINA: You promised me you'd do this.

GRUSHENKA: I don't recall any promises.

KATERINA: I can't have misunderstood you.

GRUSHENKA: You're so noble and so trusting my dear sweet lady, I ought to take your hand and kiss it 300 times. I really ought to. But I don't want to.

KATERINA: You're a slut.

GRUSHENKA: And you're a tart. Dmitry told me.

KATERINA: You're a bitch. A lying bitch, and I'll strangle you, you whore, if you lay a finger on him, I promise you –

*SMERDYAKOV slips out of GRUSHENKA into song.*

SMERDYAKOV: Love I love you
    I'll love you always
    but I am leaving
    don't weep for me.

SMERDYAKOV/IVAN/DMITRY: Oh Lord listen
    and bless my darling
    for none is lovely as she –
    none is lovely as she!

SMERDYAKOV/IVAN/DMITRY/ALYOSHA: *(Sing and dance.)*
    Love I love you
    I'll love you always
    but I am leaving
    don't weep for me.

    Oh Lord listen
    and bless my darling
    for none is lovely as she –
    none is lovely as she!

*Dance gathers momentum. DMITRY has the coat. At the climax of the dance, he whirls it around him.*

    Love I love you
    I'll love you always
    but I am leaving
    don't weep for me.

    Oh Lord listen
    and bless my darling
    for none is lovely as she –
    none is lovely as she!

*At end of dance, all collapse into separate areas, DMITRY/ KARAMAZOV enveloped in the coat.*

KARAMAZOV/DMITRY: I've made up my mind. I'm going to live till I'm 80. You won't get a penny. I'll have spent it. On her. And others like her. I'll buy them. And the older you get, the more it costs. That's why I'm rich. If I'm sick, I buy health. If I'm old, I buy youth. If I'm dying, I buy life, and more life, and more life...

IVAN: If I suddenly woke up and knew for sure that life was a sham and love was dead and the world was lost; if I was suddenly stunned by the horrors of disillusion – I'd be relieved, I'd breathe, I'd reach for the cup and raise it to my lips and drain it, every drop, to the dregs.

ALYOSHA: What's the matter Smerdyakov?

SMERDYAKOV: It's Mr Ivan sir. He's going away.

ALYOSHA: Has he told you?

SMERDYAKOV: I can feel it. I know I shouldn't. It's irrational and that's absurd. That's why I'm frightened.

ALYOSHA: He mustn't go just now.

SMERDYAKOV: You must stop him sir. He's a genius. He knows the answer.

ALYOSHA: What answer?

SMERDYAKOV: Two and two make four. He's proved it. Don't laugh sir. It's vital! As long as I can cling to the truth of that equation, I can live. But he's going away. I can feel it. It's all wrong... *(Weeps.)*

KARAMAZOV: *(To Alyosha.)* What are you staring at? Ashamed of filth? It's delicious. You should try it. Everyone shouts it down, but they're all at it on the sly. I do it openly. That's why they attack me. They're jealous. No Paradise for me. But I've got my paradise. Up to my nose in it. Sticky and sweet. You should try it boy...

IVAN: The blue sky, the green sticky leaves, the human brain, what are they for? We know what they're made of. The parts can be stripped and laid in rows. But the whole is a mystery. It fills the cup. I'm going to Europe. I know it's a graveyard lined with bones, but what bones, what a graveyard! We must meet and drink before I'm thirty, before I open my eyes.

SMERDYAKOV: You know that man sir, the one in the story, who took a four-year-old child at Eastertime and cut off his fingers and nailed him to the wall. You know the one sir?

ALYOSHA: No, and I don't want to.

SMERDYAKOV: I often dream I'm that man sir, sitting there watching for four hours and eating stewed pineapples. I'm very partial to stewed pineapples, and I know sir, that as long as I can retain that partiality, and not be put off by the moans, I'll be all right sir, according to Mr Ivan.

KARAMAZOV: Don't be fooled by Ivan. He's not clever. He's an abacus. You can hear him rattling. 35,000 to be got if I'm murdered, and if Dmitry does it, he loses his share, so that's another 17,500, and if he can pick up Katerina, there's a further 60,000. Sub-total: 112,500. He's like me. He knows money is the root of all filth. That's why he's here. He's watching, to pick me clean, like a vulture.

ALYOSHA: Ivan wait! *(Goes to him.)* What about Mitya and father?

IVAN: I'm not my brother's keeper.

ALYOSHA: Do you want father to be killed?

IVAN: We can wish what we like little brother.

ALYOSHA: You came to help us.

IVAN: I came to watch two reptiles devour each other. Curiosity, nothing more.

ALYOSHA: I don't believe that. You love life.

IVAN: That's why I'm leaving. Don't be alarmed little monk. I accept that God is good, and his design is wonderful and quite beyond our comprehension, and that man needs and fears God like a father. I find all that amazing and quite acceptable. It's the creation I stumble at: this awful morass that bears no resemblance to the original design. Is it our fault or God's that we can't live up to his impossible standards? Let's talk stupidly Alyosha. What should we do: deny our nature and disown the world, or follow our instincts and disown God?

ALYOSHA: We should love the world.

IVAN: How?

ALYOSHA: Love your neighbour. Actively and without ceasing.

*Pause.*

IVAN: There was once a boy of eight who threw a stone at a general's dog and made it lame. So the general took him and locked him up, and in the morning had him stripped and sent naked into the snow. "Make him run!" said the general, and set the dogs on him, the whole pack, which hunted the child and tore him to pieces. What judgment would you pass on the general, Alyosha? Do you shoot him? Or do you love him? Come on little brother, he's your neighbour.

ALYOSHA: Shoot him.

IVAN: Bravo!

ALYOSHA: But that's wrong!

IVAN: So there is a devil in you after all.

ALYOSHA: We have to learn to forgive.

IVAN: But the child is dead. You can't forgive on his behalf.

ALYOSHA: Only through forgiveness can we see God.

IVAN: Then I won't be seeing him, I'm sorry. If one child has to suffer so that I, through showing mercy, may gain admission to eternal life, then I decline the offer. I renounce harmony. Don't misunderstand me little brother. It's not God that I'm rejecting. I am simply, and most respectfully, handing back my ticket. *(Starts to go.)*

ALYOSHA: That's rebellion.

SMERDYAKOV: You stay with us sir.

KARAMAZOV: Ivan I want you to go to Chermashnya. I've got some business there.

ALYOSHA: There *is* an answer Ivan. There is one who can forgive!

SMERDYAKOV: If you go sir, I'll have a fit.

KARAMAZOV: You'll only be gone two or three days. It's not much to ask.

SMERDYAKOV: I promise you sir. I can feel it coming.

ALYOSHA: The one who took the blame for all the suffering in the world! He can forgive everyone and everything for ever!

IVAN: *(Turns.)* He was the cause of it all!

*SMERDYAKOV detains Ivan by robing him in the cloak and setting ALYOSHA on his knees before him.*

SMERDYAKOV: Haven't you read his poem sir? The Grand Inquisitor? Spain – the Inquisition – heretics – bonfires! Jesus comes back. The Inquisitor, age 90, with shrivelled face and sunken eyes, catches Jesus preaching in front of the cathedral. Can't allow that! Arrest him! Lock him up! There's a bonfire tomorrow. Jesus Christ will be on it!

*The GRAND INQUISITOR/IVAN addresses ALYOSHA as christ.*

INQUISITOR: What do you want? Why are you here? You did what you had to do fifteen hundred years ago. It was brief and incomplete. Caused a great deal of trouble. We are now putting it right. We don't want interference. We have authority from you, confirmed in writing, to bring people into line. If you are thinking now of withdrawing this authority, and setting man free to do as he likes, then I have no alternative but to explode this notion and repeat to you in the strongest terms, the warnings that were put to you in the wilderness. These warning, dismissed by you as frivolous temptations, were cries from the heart of a superior spirit, and together sum up all that has been written before and since your time, on the subject of man's struggle to stay alive. We have acted on these warnings, in good faith, and with spectacular results. We cannot allow our work to be undermined.

You were told first of all, to turn stones into bread. You were going into the world, with no following and no mandate, to save it from chaos. You needed the attention and obedience of mankind. You were offered the power to have them queuing for food! Yet all you could say was: "Man does not live by bread alone." The chaos of the world is rooted in *need*! You said: "Follow me and turn from sin, and I will give you the bread of heaven." There *is* no sin! Only hungry people! Feed them first, *then* demand virtue! And as for your promise of heavenly bread, this was callous in the extreme, implying that man must compete for salvation, and precipitating him into a disorderly scramble, for a substance that might mean something to a mystic on a mountain, but to the vast mass of the human race, was moonshine! Man needs to see a caring godhead, dispensing tangible, edible food, with fairness and authority. He doesn't want freedom. He wants happiness, security.

You were then taken and set on the pinnacle of the Temple and asked to throw yourself off, "for it is written, his angels shall bear thee up and thou shalt prove how great is God and how puny is man". To which you replied: "All men are divine and don't need cheap miracles to remind them of the fact." Have you looked at man? Have you asked him what he wants? He needs proof. He yearns for the suspension of the law of gravity. Otherwise he invents his own miracles and terrifies himself with sorcery and the occult. "If thou be the Son of God, come down from the cross!" But you stayed there. One transfiguration was enough. A split-second on a mountain-top before the elite of your apostles, and even *they* didn't understand it! No god can save the world if he underplays his divinity; which is why we have been at great pains to proclaim that your first mission was unfinished, and one day you will return, in chariots of fire, trailing clouds of glory. Of course you won't do this, and we don't want you to, but people need to believe. Hope has no meaning if you fulfil it. Miracle, mystery and authority: these are the principles that constitute the church. We don't want you back now, in any shape or form, tampering with these principles and confusing people.

Which brings me to the third and most urgent plea. The spirit showed you the kingdoms of the world. All these will be yours if you accept the equation of religion and politics. You rejected it, so we took it up. Man needs one faith, one law, one government. If you don't give him this, he seeks him for himself, littering history with Tamberlaines and Genghis Khans, and soaking the earth in needless blood. You showed him no love, no understanding. You set him free to run wild like a mad beast. We have tamed the beast and sat on its back, like the whore that raises the cup of mystery, of whom it is written: "The weak shall rise up and rend her purple, and strip her vile body!" May that day never come! For we know the secret. The cup that the world in its innocence craves – is *empty*! The millions upon millions whom you cast out, have come running to us, to surrender their freedom, in the simple hope that, under our care, they may live in peace, and die without terror. They know that in your grace, they will enter eternal life. We know that is a lie, and even if it were not, we know they would have no place in your selective heaven. You made it plain that only the elite may find true joy. I challenge that judgment! I too am a saint! I too fed on locusts and roots in the wilderness. I saw stars change course and parallel lines meet. Then I awoke and found myself in a world of bloodshed, starvation, needless misery. So I left the elite, and walked the earth, and strove ninety years to correct your work! Judge me if you dare! I dare to judge you!

*IVAN drops the cloak, smiles.*

ALYOSHA: Does Christ reply?

IVAN: He walks up and kisses him gently on his bloodless lips.

ALYOSHA: And the old man?

IVAN: He is moved, but he sticks to his ideas. Don't take it seriously. It's just a poem.

ALYOSHA: How can you live with such torment inside you?

IVAN: I'm a Karamazov.

ALYOSHA: You'll kill yourself.

IVAN: I shall drink the cup till I'm thirty, then dash it to the floor. And if ever I feel unloved or sick at heart, I shall think of you little brother, and your hold on life.

ALYOSHA: *(Goes up to IVAN and kisses him on the lips.)*

IVAN: *(Laughs.)* That's plagiarism. *(Moves to go.)*

SMERDYAKOV: *(To IVAN.)* If you have to go sir, please go to Chermashnya, not Moscow. It's nearer. It's Mr Dmitry. He'll kill me, grind me in a mortar. I'll have a fit tomorrow, I know it: a long one, a really serious epileptic fit sir – like when I fell from the loft. I was out for three days. Only this time it'll be the cellar. It's not a trick sir, and if it *was* and I faked it, which I can sir, I'd be entitled to fake it, to save my skin…

ALYOSHA: I've got to go father.

KARAMAZOV/DMITRY: Stay here tonight.

ALYOSHA: The elder is dying. I promised I'd be with him.

KARAMAZOV: She'll come tonight. Ivan's leaving, I'm sending him away. If you're here, we can have some fun, and Dmitry won't kill me. He couldn't kill me if you were here.

ALYOSHA: I'm leaving you father. The elder's dying.

KARAMAZOV: *I'm* dying boy! You're responsible for *me*!

SMERDYAKOV: *(To IVAN.)* Grushenka will come and Dmitry will kill your father, and you'll be to blame because you're not here to stop it!

*IVAN has gone.*

DMITRY: *(Strips off the coat and thrusts it into ALYOSHA's hands.)* Stay with him Alyosha. I couldn't kill him if you were there. I'll find the money somewhere else. 3000, by tomorrow night, I'll find it! *(Runs off.)*

*SMERDYAKOV approaches ALYOSHA, takes the coat from him and slowly dresses him in it.*

SMERDYAKOV: They've all deserted you sir. You mustn't worry. They've all gone. Except me. I'm your son sir, your own flesh, the only one who truly loves you.

KARAMAZOV/ALYOSHA: Grushenka...

SMERDYAKOV: She'll come tonight sir. It's all clear. Ivan's gone. I knew he would.

KARAMAZOV: Grushenka...

SMERDYAKOV: He left an hour ago. On the Moscow train.

KARAMAZOV: Grushenka... Grushenka... Grushenka...

IVAN: *(Alone.)* I was eleven. With my grandmother, staying by the railway. Kids in the village. I was the youngest. Used to sneak out at night. Play on the line. Lie down between the rails! Let the train pass right over! You couldn't, you wouldn't dare. We had a bet: two roubles. I lay down between the rails. The eleven o'clock was due. The others ran back. I lay there waiting. The signals changed. The kids shouted: Run! It's coming! The train came thundering...

*SMERDYAKOV screaming tumbles in violent epileptic fit which lasts the length of ALYOSHA's song.*

ALYOSHA: *(Sings.)*
All his fiery wounds
now bleed anew!
Through his soul,
hell's bitter torments run!
Father, cries the youth,
I'm killing you!
And the father's heart
hath whispered: Son...

*End of Act One*

# ACT TWO

## THE QUADRILLION KILOMETRES

*(The dead ZOSIMA/SMERDYAKOV laid out in the cloak. ALYOSHA kneels before the bier. Ivan stands behind him.)*

ALYOSHA: *(Sings.)*
    Ice cold ice cold
    in his shroud he lies.
    All thy gentle sweetest
    dreams have burst.

    Sweet and gentle
    father thou art curst.
    Ice cold ice cold
    in his shroud he lies.

    *Speaks.*

    Except a corn of wheat fall into the ground and die, it abideth alone. But if it die, it bringeth forth much fruit.

IVAN: He stinks. ZOSIMA was a fake…

ALYOSHA: Oh Lord bless the soul of thy sleeping saint…

IVAN: His faith was unsound. His love was sensual…

ALYOSHA: Give me faith to believe in the miracle of his death…

IVAN: He was not strict in fasting. He took cherry jam with his tea…

ALYOSHA: My love is weak. I have no strength to destroy my doubts…

IVAN: What is faith: a rock, or a drug? If it's a rock and you cling to it as you fall into the pit, all it can do is drag you down faster. If it's a drug, how do you know it won't wear off?

ALYOSHA: Sow the seed in his people and it will not die…

IVAN: He sat in pride. He seduced the faithful…

ALYOSHA: Love their faith and God's kingdom will be…

IVAN: They judged him a saint, but God has clothed him in the stench of Satan…

ALYOSHA: It will be! It will be!

IVAN: Cast him out! Cast him out!

ALYOSHA: I did believe! I do believe! I want to believe! *(Falls to the ground.)*

*"Over Barren Blackened Earth" is hummed as ZOSIMA speaks.*

ZOSIMA: *(Sits up.)* Hear me my son. There was once a wicked woman who died, and the angels could not recall one good deed which might save her soul. So the devils took her and threw her into the lake of fire. But her guardian angel suddenly recalled that once long ago she had given an onion to a beggar. So God said: "Take the onion and hold it over the burning lake. Let her grasp it and if you can pull her out, she shall be saved and come to Paradise. So diligent and strong is the mercy of God, that a soul needs only one godly deed to assure him of the goal of faith. *(Lies down.)*

IVAN: May I finish the story? The onion was held over the burning lake. The woman grasped it. The angel pulled. But the other lost souls didn't want to be left out. So they clung to the woman who kicked them off: "It's *my* onion! *Mine!*" Whereupon it broke and she fell back in, and she's sizzling to this day.

ALYOSHA: Oh Lord you have judged your saint to be false and have defiled his body with the stench of this world. I have no strength to rouse me from the pit. Your jealous wrath has damned mankind, and there is no redemption.

*DMITRY appears singing softly "love, I love you…" and dancing as if in a trance. His shirt and his raised hands are steeped in blood. He is clutching fistfuls of rainbow-coloured notes. Ivan raises ALYOSHA and together they dispose of the dead ZOSIMA.*

IVAN: Enjoy yourself to the very dregs until you're thirty. Then you have a choice. Fling away the cup and die while you're drunk, or place it on a high shelf and comfort your fellow men by lying to them that it's still full. As a thinking man who cares for the world, I suggest you do the latter.

*They set the scene for the interrogation.*

Work out a system, whereby the things you like may flourish and things you don't like may be controlled. Call the first group Right and the second group Wrong. For instance: love is right; anger is wrong. Duty is right; parricide is wrong. Then go to the people with your manifesto. Lie to them that it's the word of God. Persuade them to lay down their freedom in exchange for order and happiness.

*They notice DMITRY.*

IVAN: What's the matter with you?

DMITRY: I'm in heaven!

ALYOSHA: Have you been in a fight?

IVAN: What's all this money?

DMITRY: It's mine. I'm spending it.

ALYOSHA: You're covered in blood.

DMITRY: I ran over an old woman. We had a fight. He didn't understand me.

IVAN: He?

DMITRY: An old man. It was an old man. We've made it up – best of friends!

ALYOSHA: Father has been murdered.

DMITRY: What?

ALYOSHA: His skull was broken. They've found the weapon.

IVAN: 3000 roubles were taken.

DMITRY: When?

IVAN: Last night.

DMITRY: That's nonsense. I saw him

ALYOSHA: When?

DMITRY: Last night.

IVAN: What were you doing?

DMITRY: I was in the garden.

ALYOSHA: What time?

DMITRY: I don't know. About midnight.

IVAN: That's when he was murdered.

DMITRY: Murdered!

ALYOSHA: Can you tell us what you've been doing since yesterday morning?

DMITRY: You'd better tell *me*. But gently, I haven't slept. I've drunk the ocean.

IVAN: Do you mind if I take some notes?

DMITRY: Go ahead.

ALYOSHA: He was found lying on the floor of his bedroom with his head battered in.

DMITRY: God…

ALYOSHA: There was an empty envelope beside him. The back door was open.

DMITRY: No it was closed. I remember it was closed.

IVAN: Can you tell us what you were doing in the garden?

DMITRY: What is this, an interrogation?

IVAN: There are several factors which all tend towards one conclusion.

DMITRY: Namely what?

IVAN: Let's start from the beginning.

DMITRY: Best place.

IVAN: Your attitude over the past week or so.

DMITRY: What attitude?

IVAN: Towards father.

DMITRY: I hated him. That's not an attitude.

ALYOSHA: And you declared in public, on several occasions that you wanted to kill him.

DMITRY: He owed me money. 28,000. What are you writing?

IVAN: And you needed 3000 immediately.

DMITRY: Are you adding two and two? What do you make it? 7? 13? 29?

ALYOSHA: Can you tell us what you've been doing since yesterday morning?

DMITRY: Certainly not.

IVAN: It's in your own interests.

DMITRY: I'm not falling for that one.

ALYOSHA: We need every detail.

DMITRY: "What did you have for breakfast? Where did you go? Who did you talk to? Who did you murder?" It's a trick you see. You sneak up on me with irrelevant questions, and catch me out! *(Laughs.)* I'm not falling for that.

ALYOSHA: You've got to help us.

DMITRY: I *am* helping you! God in heaven, can't I make a joke? You think I'm drunk.

IVAN: If you're innocent, you'll want to get to the bottom of this –

DMITRY: *If* I'm innocent! Innocent of what?

IVAN: You came here covered in blood, clutching fistfuls of money –

DMITRY: Holy Saviour! What do you want? I've told you: I didn't do it! I didn't do it! My head…

ALYOSHA: Do you want some water?

DMITRY: No. Sorry. I haven't slept… And if you want to know what I had for breakfast, I haven't had anything. That's why I'm feeling so raw. I'm sorry… You shouldn't have jumped on me. I wasn't expecting it… So he's dead… All right. Let's get on with it. But on one condition: that you treat me like an officer. I know I'm *not* an officer, but I *was* an officer and I would like to be treated *like* an officer.

IVAN: We would like you to behave like an officer.

DMITRY: So what have I been up to?

ALYOSHA: Since yesterday morning.

DMITRY: Let's see. I had a mission: a financial matter, which I won't go into because it's irrelevant – concerning the sum of 3000 roubles, which I had to find at very short notice. You were right about that.

ALYOSHA: You know that father kept precisely that sum under his pillow?

DMITRY: Which is why I went to Samsonov. I'm not a ferret who pokes about under old men's pillows. I go straight in and confront him head-on. You know Samsonov, very rich, semi-retired, lives at the far end of town, like a bloated dragon. Well I'm St George, and I ride straight in to rescue the peerless beauty who's been going to him regularly once a week for the past five years, and he hasn't touched her! She just goes to do his accounts. And I believe her. She's an angel, and she's mine. We were bound last night by one immortal cord that will never be broken, never, *never*! What are you writing?

IVAN: Just notes.

DMITRY: Are they relevant? I don't want you writing down anything that isn't relevant.

IVAN: Perhaps if you confined what you have to say –

DMITRY: To what is relevant –

IVAN: It would make it easier.

DMITRY: Much easier.

ALYOSHA: So you went to see Samsonov.

DMITRY: And I put my scheme to him, which is irrelevant,
so I won't go into it, except to say that the village of
Chermashnya is morally mine, having been extracted by
father from my mother's estate, and I'm about to, or *was*
about to, initiate proceedings against him regarding the
title, and my purpose in visiting Samsonov was to tell him
of my interest in Chermashnya, which had been priced
conservatively at 28,000, and I was offering it for 3! But he
wasn't interested. He hasn't been well. In fact he's dying.
Everyone's dying. Or dead. Except me. I keep going. I
can't accept the logic of death. I ride on. I don't give up.
So Samsonov puts me on to Lyagavy, or Gorskin as he's
correctly known, not a local man, but as luck would have
it, he was staying with a priest at Ilyinskoye. So I took a
carriage to Volovya station – had to sell my watch to pay
for it! It's a silver one, had it for ages, and all I got was six
roubles. It was worth 20, but I didn't have time to argue,
because I was late, but I didn't know it till I got to Volovya,
not having a watch. I hate watches! Time is a tyrant and
my mission is to destroy him, as I did last night!

IVAN: But this is all by the way.

DMITRY: You asked for everything in detail.

ALYOSHA: I don't think we need all the details.

DMITRY: Well you're getting them. I'm sorry, where was I?

IVAN: Somewhere between Volovya and Ilyinskoye.

DMITRY: I was lost, hopelessly lost, and when I found the
place, the priest said he's just gone to Sukhoy Possyolok
to buy some timber. Well I hadn't come all that way to
be sold a mare's nest, so I dragged the little priest five
miles on foot to find Lyagavy, or Gorskin as he's correctly
known, though as it turned out, he wouldn't have cared if
I'd called him the devil's backside, which I'd a good mind
to, because when we got there, he was fast asleep, dead

drunk, couldn't wake him. So I left him and came back, feeling pretty sore as you can imagine.

IVAN: What time was this?

DMITRY: Mid-afternoon.

ALYOSHA: What did you do then?

DMITRY: I went to Mrs Khokhlakova. Wealthy widow, fall for anything. "Mrs K, I've got a scheme. Can't fail, make you 25,000, overnight!" But she was in a trance. "Siberia… Goldmines…That's where the money is. Find me a goldmine and I'll give you 3,000…" 3,000! I'll find you a hundred goldmines! Just give me the money. *(Lying.)* So she did. And that's it, what's left of it. I've spent most of it.

IVAN: You got this money from Mrs Khokhlakova.

DMITRY: Yes.

ALYOSHA: 3,000?

DMITRY: 3,000.

IVAN: Will she confirm this?

DMITRY: You think I'm lying.

ALYOSHA: You are lying.

DMITRY: Yes I am, and it's irrelevant. What are you writing?

IVAN: That it's relevant.

DMITRY: You don't deserve to listen to me. You think I'm a petty thief.

IVAN: You're under suspicion.

DMITRY: What *for*? What motive?

IVAN: Jealousy.

DMITRY: Jealousy!

IVAN: You were jealous of the old man's attachment to Grushenka.

DMITRY: "Othello is not jealous, he is *trustful.*" His ideal has been destroyed. I am *trustful* of Grushenka. I trust her to be loyal. So when I go to her and she isn't there, my ideal is in ruins! She's with *him*! She's gone to *him*! For the money! I go mad! I race to the house, leap the fence, run through the garden, and there he is, sitting in the window, waiting. She isn't there. Thank God she isn't there! And I hate him. *(Seething.)* Suddenly I hate his fat little face, the fleshy bags under his eyes, his teeth, his slack lips, and his adam's apple dangling like a purse! *(Pause.)* What's that stone in your ring?

IVAN: A topaz. What's that got to do with it?

DMITRY: Nothing.

ALYOSHA: The pestle. You had a brass pestle.

DMITRY: I picked it up.

ALYOSHA: Why?

DMITRY: I was in a hurry.

IVAN: What did you want it for?

DMITRY: To keep off the dogs. They chase me, in the dark. Will you write that down?

IVAN: So you were standing by the window with the pestle. Did he see you?

DMITRY: He came to the window and looked right out.

IVAN: What happened then?

DMITRY: I murdered him. Don't write that down, it's irrelevant.

IVAN: *(Angry.)* Take this seriously!

DMITRY: Two twos are four!

IVAN: We want the truth!

ALYOSHA: What really happened?

DMITRY: My dead mother fell at the feet of God and begged him to send my guardian angel to me, who shot down like a bolt, and caught my arm and flung me to the fence!

IVAN: The servant Grigory said you came out of the house.

DMITRY: He's dead. Grigory's dead.

ALYOSHA: He said the back door was open.

DMITRY: It was shut, and he's dead.

IVAN: He's not dead.

DMITRY: I killed him! I was climbing the fence. He grabbed my leg, couldn't shake him off, so I killed him!

ALYOSHA: He survived.

DMITRY: I hit him – like that! His face…and the blood! I tried to wipe him. The blood…

ALYOSHA: He's not dead.

DMITRY: He was a father to me. The fool, the fool!

IVAN: He's the principal witness against you.

DMITRY: He's dead!

IVAN: He said the door was open.

DMITRY: It was shut!

ALYOSHA: He's not dead. You didn't kill him. He's alive. He was found crawling towards the cottage. He survived.

DMITRY: So I'm clean…

IVAN: We'll have to examine your clothes.

DMITRY: Tell Grushenka, I'm clean. I'm clean!

ALYOSHA: Where did you go when you left the garden?

DMITRY: *(Sings.)* Glory to God in the highest! Glory to God in *me*!

IVAN: May we have your coat?

DMITRY: *(Taking off jacket.)* Tell her to open the champagne! I ordered 48 bottles!

ALYOSHA: You went back to Grushenka's, but she wasn't there.

DMITRY: And cheeses, Strasbourg pies, smoked whitefish, caviare –

ALYOSHA: Her servant said you had a bundle of rainbow notes.

DMITRY: I spent 300 roubles!

IVAN: Your belt please.

ALYOSHA: Where did you get the money?

DMITRY: *(Taking off belt.)* And ten on the boy and 30 on the carriage.

ALYOSHA: You went to Mokroye –

DMITRY: She'd gone there with her officer who loved her five years ago. But I was trustful, so trustful! I raced through the night!

ALYOSHA: That's 340.

DMITRY: And 200 on the gypsies. Lovely dancers!

IVAN: Your boots, we need them.

DMITRY: *(Taking off boots.)* She was there in the corner, sitting with her man. She looked tiny and so sad.

ALYOSHA: The innkeeper says you paid him 70.

DMITRY: She introduced us and you know he wasn't an army officer at all! He was a *customs* officer!

ALYOSHA: And you lost 90 at cards.

IVAN: Your shirt, may we have it please?

ALYOSHA: That makes 700 in all.

DMITRY: I'll keep my shirt.

IVAN: I'm sorry we have to have it.

DMITRY: I am an officer! I demand the courtesy of an officer!

IVAN: It's in your own interest to hand it over.

DMITRY: *(Tearing it off.)* I'm bound by money! I'm bound by petty rules and clerks and customs officers with sagging shoulders and dyed hair!

ALYOSHA: You had quite a celebration. Everyone's talking about it.

DMITRY: And he wasn't even Russian. He was a Pole! And she hated him. He'd shrunk over five years into a spineless worm and a miserable disappointment. She was so relieved when I came in. Her face lit up! She was my queen!

IVAN: And your trousers please.

ALYOSHA: How much did you have with you when you left the inn?

DMITRY: *(Removing trousers.)* I don't know. Count them. It's all there. And keep it. It's not mine.

ALYOSHA: *(Counting.)* Whose is it?

DMITRY: I can't tell you

ALYOSHA: It's in your own interest.

DMITRY: I stole it.

ALYOSHA: Who from?

DMITRY: I'm a thief.

IVAN: Your socks please.

DMITRY: Don't tell Grushenka. I hugged her for an hour. Don't tell her I'm a thief.

ALYOSHA: There's 800 here. With the money you spent, that makes 1500.

IVAN: And your underclothes. We need everything.

DMITRY: All gone.

ALYOSHA: Where's the other 1500?

*DMITRY removes the last of his clothes. He sits hunched up, all dignity lost.*

DMITRY: That's all I had. It's all gone… I held her for an hour, and she's gone… She's all I had… I was going to kill myself, blow my brains out. I even wrote a note. It's in my pocket. "I'm punishing my life. My whole life I punish." I was going to look at the bullet, load it, and blow my brains out. But I'd pawned my pistols… Grushenka had a knife. I was going to slit my throat. I hugged her for an hour, shut my eyes… and we were jolting in a cart, down a long street to the town square. I could see the scaffold, the sun behind it, and the birds soaring… bright blue sky… miles away. The street was lined with laughing faces, pointing and shouting, little children running, and the houses full of daily noise, inching by. A long way to go, a whole life to live, before we got to the square. A whole age to live as we came nearer to the end…every jolt of the cart, every cobble in the road, all different, and then gone… and always more… We rode for hours, many days, in the black cart… and she wasn't there. The road was rough, straggled houses, burnt black, charred beams reaching out… and the people staring. No sound, except the rain, the freezing rain. They stood in groups, haggard and thin… no movement, not a sound, staring with huge eyes, as the rain poured down. I saw a woman, with a naked child, crying at her breast, little fists clenched and blue with cold. Why don't you feed him? Why is he crying? Why is the babby crying? Why is the babby crying…?

*IVAN visits SMERDYAKOV.*

IVAN: How are you Smerdyakov?

SMERDYAKOV: Very poorly sir, thank you for asking.

IVAN: You've had a severe attack.

SMERDYAKOV: I nearly died. Ten recurrences. I was out for two days. I told you I had it coming sir, didn't I? But you didn't believe me.

IVAN: One cannot foretell an epileptic fit.

SMERDYAKOV: One can have a presentiment sir.

IVAN: How did it happen?

SMERDYAKOV: Well, like I said sir, it was down the cellar. I knew it would be the cellar, because last time it was the loft.

IVAN: You can't have known it would be the cellar.

SMERDYAKOV: Excuse me but I did sir. As I was going down I felt it. I was terrified. "I'm going to have a fit. I'm <u>sure</u> I'll have a fit. And Mr Ivan's run away. And Mr Dmitry'll come –"

IVAN: You faked it.

SMERDYAKOV: Oh sir!

IVAN: You said you could fake it and you did.

SMERDYAKOV: How can you <u>say</u> that?

IVAN: You knew something would happen and you wanted to be out of the way.

SMERDYAKOV: Not me sir! Oh no sir!

IVAN: You told me that before I left.

SMERDYAKOV: That was for your benefit sir.

IVAN: What do you mean by that?

SMERDYAKOV: Well sir, I thought, with you running off so suddenly, if something *did* happen sir, which could have been prevented if you'd stayed, I thought the blame for such an occurrence might reasonably attach itself to you sir, on account of your absence being calculated to facilitate the occurrence, bearing in mind also sir, what you stood to gain from your father's decease, if I may put it so obliquely sir, and without offence.

IVAN: I ought to thrash you for this.

SMERDYAKOV: Go ahead sir. I'm a sick man. I've got pains in all my limbs. You ask the doctors sir. It was like a hundred whips and scorpions –

IVAN: Very well, I won't say anything.

SMERDYAKOV: About what sir?

IVAN: About your capacity to fake an attack.

SMERDYAKOV: That's very civil of you sir.

IVAN: And I advise you not to say anything about it either.

SMERDYAKOV: I won't sir. Nor will I allude in any way to the circumstances of you running off when you did sir.

*He hums "Love, I love you" under the following scene.*

*ALYOSHA puts a blanket round DMITRY, then with a bowl, water and a cloth, silently bathes his face and hands. Silence.*

DMITRY: There's a new man within me and I never knew… It was the shock of the lightning… Why did I dream about the babby…? It's for the babby I have to go down into the mines for twenty years… I did not kill my father, but I've got to go down into the tear-drenched earth… for all the babbies…

*IVAN visits SMERDYAKOV.*

SMERDYAKOV: *(With a book.)* Nice to see you again sir.

IVAN: How are you feeling Smerdyakov?

SMERDYAKOV: One the mend sir, thank you for asking. Provided I don't excite myself.

IVAN: What are you studying?

SMERDYAKOV: I'm learning French sir.

IVAN: What use is that to you?

SMERDYAKOV: Improves the mind sir. Also I'm a cook sir, *et la langue particuliere de la cuisine…*

IVAN: What did you mean when you said you wouldn't tell anyone about the circumstances of my departure?

SMERDYAKOV: Which departure sir?

IVAN: Before my father died.

SMERDYAKOV: What did I mean sir?

IVAN: You seemed to imply that I was in some way responsible.

SMERDYAKOV: Well you were sir.

IVAN: I didn't kill him.

SMERDYAKOV: I think you did sir.

IVAN: How could I kill him? I wasn't even there!

SMERDYAKOV: Precisely sir. You're a clever man. Got someone else to do it.

IVAN: *(Laughs.)* The rubbish I put up with from you!

SMERDYAKOV: *(Laughs.)* It's funny isn't it sir?

IVAN: You killed him.

SMERDYAKOV: I was laid up!

IVAN: You faked it.

SMERDYAKOV: I'm not that clever sir. I'm clever enough to see what *your* motive would be, but I'm hanged if I know what I'd do it for!

IVAN: What's my motive?

SMERDYAKOV: 35,000 sir. And if Dmitry is convicted, a further 17,500. Not to mention the 60,000 you could get from Miss Katerina if you played your cards right. And you're well into that game aren't you sir? Wooing her like a turkey-cock, so rumour has it –

IVAN: *(Hitting him.)* You bastard!

SMERDYAKOV: *(Cringing under the blows.)* Yes I am sir! And my mother was a loony! They scraped me up off the bath-house slime! I'm a poor bastard lackey, but I'm clever enough to know sir, that I've got your protection, and I'll have it all my life sir, because I wouldn't tell anyone how you got your inheritance, so long as it was used to protect me and support me, on an arrangement that can be formalized at our mutual convenience, if that's all right by you, Mr Karamazov?

*ALYOSHA brings clean clothes for DMITRY. Helps him dress.*

ALYOSHA: The money, where is it?

DMITRY: I spent it.

ALYOSHA: The 3000.

DMITRY: I stole it.

ALYOSHA: You spent 1500.

DMITRY: I had 3000. I'm a thief.

ALYOSHA: Where's the rest?

DMITRY: But not a murderer.

ALYOSHA: If we can prove you only had 1500 –

DMITRY: I had 3000.

ALYOSHA: What did you do with it?

DMITRY: I spent it.

ALYOSHA: You didn't, you spent only 1500.

DMITRY: I spent the other 1500.

ALYOSHA: When?

DMITRY: About a month ago.

ALYOSHA: Where did you get it?

DMITRY: I stole it.

ALYOSHA: Who from?

*Pause.*

DMITRY: Katerina. She gave me 3000 to send to her sister in
    Moscow, but I stole it.

ALYOSHA: So the money you spent the other night –

DMITRY: Was Katerina's.

ALYOSHA: Not father's.

DMITRY: It was in the bag round my neck, and as long as it
    was there, I wasn't a thief. I was going to give it back. I told
    you, remember? *(Beating his chest.)* I'm not a thief! I'm not
    a thief! I was hitting the bag!

ALYOSHA: Do you have this bag?

DMITRY: Don't you believe me?

ALYOSHA: We need proof.

DMITRY: *(Angry.)* You're like all the rest!

ALYOSHA: Ivan is bringing Smerdyakov to the trial as our principal witness –

DMITRY: Ivan thinks I'm guilty. He's proved it.

ALYOSHA: He knows it wasn't you.

DMITRY: Who was it then? Smerdyakov? He was sick. Who was it? The devil?

*IVAN visits SMERDYAKOV.*

SMERDYAKOV: How are you feeling sir? You look dreadful if you don't mind my saying. Your face, it's all puffy. And your eyes sir, they're yellow. You've not been sleeping have you sir?

IVAN: I've had things on my mind.

SMERDYAKOV: I know you have, and it's so stupid sir. I'd have told you if only you'd been straight with me.

IVAN: Told me what?

SMERDYAKOV: I've learnt so much from you sir: about the structure of the world, the laws of the universe, the mortality of the soul. You've been so good to me. Would you like some lemonade?

IVAN: No thanks.

SMERDYAKOV: You've taught me that eveything I've ever seen or heard, every notion I've entertained, every principle I've valued, is a lie, a plain lie, from beginning to end. Nothing is worth anything. There is no system. Everything is permitted. Would you help me off with my sock sir?

IVAN: *(Helping him.)* What is it, swollen ankles?

SMERDYAKOV: You could put it like that sir. I'm very sick. They probably told you – not as sick as you sir, but pretty bad all the same. Only got a few days.

IVAN: The trial's tomorrow. You'd better be all right for that.

SMERDYAKOV: The trial can take care of itself sir.

IVAN: *(Taking wad from sock.)* What's this?

SMERDYAKOV: 3000 roubles. It wasn't under his pillow; it was behind the icon. But only I was to know that sir. I faked it, the fit. You were clever enough to put your finger on that one weren't you sir?

IVAN: You killed him.

SMERDYAKOV: No, *you* killed him.

IVAN: I wasn't there.

SMERDYAKOV: Don't start that again.

IVAN: How could I kill him if I was 500 miles away?

SMERDYAKOV: You arranged it. I was simply the instrument of your design.

IVAN: Oh God...

SMERDYAKOV: You don't believe in him sir. You don't understand the power you had over me. I would have done anything for you. I would have loved you like a brother, except that would have been sentimental and your teaching forbade that. If it's any consolation sir, I didn't feel any remorse; I just hit him with a paperweight. It was like clubbing a dead sheep. Your teaching paid off sir. I had no irrational reflex. I just did it and went back to bed, forgetting to close the door I must admit, but we all make one mistake don't we sir?

IVAN: You did it for the money.

SMERDYAKOV: No sir. I just took the money, to incriminate Mr Dmitry, which I did pretty effectively you must admit sir. He hasn't a leg to stand on. He wanted to kill his father and I was expecting him to do it. I only did the job for him, because at the crucial moment, he let us down. He's so unpredictable. So if you'll take the advice of your humble servant and instrument, you'll reap where I have sown. And you don't have to concern yourself with protecting me. I'll be dead. So you just lie back and bask in the clover which I shall be pushing up, without a whisper on your conscience, because you're clever enough not to have one. *(Goes.)*

*The DEVIL/DMITRY enters in the cloak.*

DEVIL: *(Sneezes.)*

IVAN: Who are you?

DEVIL: Sorry, I've got a terrible cold.

IVAN: What do you want?

DEVIL: I transformed too early. Couldn't wait to get here. I
always look forward to these trips. Stupid really.

IVAN: You don't exist.

DEVIL: I wish I didn't! You've no idea what it's like, in the
waters above the firmament: 150 below zero! Like licking
an axe in the depths of winter. Rips your tongue off
– vicious!

IVAN: You're not welcome here.

DEVIL: I never am. Can't think why. I go out of my way to
be nice to people. I love it here. It's so geometric. With
us, everything is an indeterminate equation. Never get
anywhere.

IVAN: I'm not listening.

DEVIL: Why do I get such a bad press? All I want is to join in.
I'm a gossip. Can't stop talking. That's what I love about
the human form. It's so trivial! Can't stand spiritualists.
Keep you running up and down in horns and tails and
cloven feet, as if belief depended on material proof!

IVAN: I'm talking to myself.

DEVIL: I'm a realist, not a materialist. My one ambition is to
be reincarnated as an 16-stone housewife.

IVAN: If I walk about with a wet towel on my head –

DEVIL: I'll still be here.

IVAN: You're the side of me I don't like.

DEVIL: You should kick me. I deserve it.

IVAN: That would prove you were here.

DEVIL: So it would! They said you were clever.

IVAN: You're my illness.

DEVIL: That's a start.

IVAN: When I'm better –

DEVIL: You'll be yourself again. But until then you'll have to sit me out.

IVAN: What are you here for?

DEVIL: To negate. It's not an attractive job, because I'm basically kind-hearted, but it's necessary as you'll appreciate. Imagine what it would be like with no negation. Nothing would happen: no suspense, so surprises, no warnings, no opposition. Without the critic there is no drama. "Hosannah must be tried in the crucible of doubt." That's what we're told. Otherwise life is an endless church service: holy but dull. Not that I'd mind. I hate this job. People take me so seriously. If I was a 16-stone housewife, perhaps they'd see the funny side. But then they wouldn't suffer, and they have to suffer, or else how would they know pleasure? I am the "x" in the indeterminate equation. I have no beginning, no end, no name, no address. Cheer me up, I'm getting morbid.

IVAN: Have you ever seen God?

DEVIL: I don't know. Have you?

IVAN: You're me, so you haven't.

DEVIL: I know someone who has.

IVAN: Who's that?

DEVIL: He was like you. Repudiated everything: conscience, faith, after-life – all eyewash! When you go – bang, nothing, the end. Well he died, and you can imagine how furious he was to find before him, the whole expanse of eternity. "This is against my principles!" he said, and for that he was condemned to walk the long dark road for a quadrillion kilometres – did you know we've gone metric? – a quadrillion, no less! After which the gates of heaven would be opened and his sins would be forgiven. Well he stood there seething. "I won't do it! I refuse!" And he lay down in the middle of the road, and stayed there for a thousand years, after which he got up and started walking. A billion years later, he reached the gates and went in, and before he had been there two seconds, he cried out: "For this I would have walked a quadrillion of quadrillions to the quadrillionth power! And he sang Hosannah with such enthusiasm that a number of the saints would not shake hands with him at first –

IVAN: That's *my* story! I wrote it when I was seventeen.

DEVIL: So you did.

IVAN: Which proves you don't exist.

DEVIL: Oh dear so it does.

IVAN: You're a dream.

DEVIL: And you don't believe in me?

IVAN: Not in a hundredth part of you.

DEVIL: A thousandth part? A ten thousandth part?

IVAN: Much as I'd like to, I can't.

DEVIL: Much as you'd *like* to! Ha *ha*!

IVAN: You're not here –

DEVIL: I've got you! It was a trick you see. As long as you were dangling between belief and disbelief, it was torture for both of us. I couldn't get a hold. But now that you're empty and pure of all doubt, I can sow in you the tiniest grain of faith, which will grow into an oak-tree, beneath which you can sit, like the hermits in the wilderness, saving your soul in a seventh heaven of peace.

IVAN: You're not here to do good.

DEVIL: Let me explain. I negate. I am the minus sign and in negating your negation, I make a plus! I do good! It's so rare I get the chance for it. And with the author of The Grand Inquisitor and the The Geological Cataclysm –

*Knocking starts.*

IVAN: I've got a head-ache.

DEVIL: I am your head-ache.

IVAN: Go away!

DEVIL: I'm right in there behind your eyes, directing them like lanterns down the quadrillion kilometre road. What was it you said in The Geological Cataclysm?

IVAN: I said nothing need be destroyed but the idea of God.

DEVIL: Go on.

IVAN: Then men will unite in one brotherhood –

DEVIL: To what end?

IVAN: To get everything possible from life as it is now, without the pressure of having to save up for the hereafter –

DEVIL: And what will happen?

IVAN: Man will become man-god, instead of man-slave and a new age will dawn.

DEVIL: When? When will it happen?

IVAN: When man has the courage to kick God from his head.

DEVIL: Will it happen overnight?

IVAN: I don't know, probably not.

DEVIL: What if it happens only gradually?

IVAN: It will happen! It will happen!

DEVIL: But man is dim and rebellious. He can't take these decisions. You've said so.

IVAN: Then he must be taught.

DEVIL: By whom?

IVAN: By men of courage and vision.

DEVIL: Will they force him?

IVAN: They'll teach him! He'll understand!

DEVIL: But he's dim!

IVAN: Then they'll force him!

DEVIL: But what if it takes a thousand years? What if millions of innocents die before the new age dawns? What if it *never* dawns? What if they're *wrong*?

ALYOSHA: *(Hammering on the door.)* Ivan! Ivan! Quick! Open up!

IVAN: They they're wrong! And we're damned!

*DEVIL vanishes.*

ALYOSHA: Ivan! Ivan!

IVAN: *(Letting him in.)* What is it? What do you want?

ALYOSHA: Smerdyakov hanged himself an hour ago.

*A long cry from SMERDYAKOV which becomes the first word of the song. during the song, the brothers set the scene for the trial.*

BROTHERS: *(Sing.)*
Our…

town is an average town for its size,

doesn't run to extremes or aspire to the skies,

has a law court, monastery and annual fair;

it's marked on the map but it could be anywhere.

Our…

town is an average town for its size,

doesn't run to extremes or aspire to the skies,

has a law court monastery and annual fair;

it's marked on the map but it could be anywhere.

What a…

shock then it was for our plain little town

to be plunged in the maelstrom of national renown

with the world and his wife filling every hotel!

What attraction has caused

our discreet little town

to do so well?

ALYOSHA: The trial of Dmitry Fyodorovich Karamazov!

DMITRY: I plead guilty to idleness, selfishness, drunkenness, debauchery and neglect of my fellow men, but I did not kill my father. I swear that before God.

ALYOSHA: The Prosecution!

PROSECUTION COUNSEL/SMERDYAKOV: *(Wearing the cloak.)* Gentlemen of the jury, this case has caused a sensation across the country. But what, I ask you is so horrifying about it? Are we not used to this kind of atrocity? Are we not, in our new liberal western attitudes, encouraged to be indifferent, lukewarm and cynical about the collapse of a family? What is truly horrifying surely, is that we have ceased to be horrified; that the crime of parricide should draw an audience as to a circus; that a murder of a father by his child should appear so trifling!

Let us look at this not untypical modern family, these unhappy Karamazovs whom we know so well, and discern, if we will, a warning to our modern society. The father, Fyodor Karamazov, head of the family, depraved, licentious, avaricious, raised his sons in the back yard, taught them the moral imperative of "*Apres moi, le deluge*", and then sent them packing, as soon as they could walk, so that he could enjoy unhindered the amassing of money and the gratification of his senses.

But the sons came back. Dmitry, the eldest, expelled from the army, prodigal and penniless, came back to dispute his inheritance, and quarrel with his father over a woman. Ivan, the intellectual, whose creed is that virtue does not exist, so everything is permitted, came back to observe the two reptiles devour each other. Alyosha, the young monk, who ran to the monastery to escape the terrors of freedom, came back in conscience to mediate in the quarrel.

But on the night of the murder, Ivan Karamazov took a train to Moscow; Alyosha Karamazov fled for a blessing to the breast of mother church; and Dmitry Karamazov, drunk, desperate, unimpeded, was discovered in the garden, blood-stained and clutching 3000 roubles –

DMITRY: 1500!

ALYOSHA: Silence in court!

PROSECUTION: I draw the court's attention to the actions of
the whole family, to show that this tragedy is *our* tragedy
gentlemen: no isolated crime, but the catastrophe that
must follow when the pillars of our sacred institutions
are taken away. Is it too late to reinstate them? Is it too
late gentlemen, to stop this troika that is racing to the
west, where the sanctions of history are cast aside, and
everything is permitted; where the only virtue is parricide,
for breaking the chain of ancient law; where the son is free
because the father was free, to abandon his conscience
and give rein to his will! We are hurtling to this end
gentlemen; we are racing towards Sodom, to the lure of
the marketplace where murder and misery may be bought
and sold. The world has proclaimed freedom. What is this
freedom but slavery to the senses, despair and suicide? If
you love this earth, if you grieve for it, fellow countrymen,
I beg you, hold to our traditions, rein in the troika, avenge
Karamazov, vile though he was, and show by your verdict,
that our nation will stand, rooted to the soil, while other
"free" nations leap their bounds and plunge to destruction!

DMITRY: Bravo! Bravo! Bravo!

DEFENCE COUNSEL/ALYOSHA: *(Assuming the cloak.)*
Gentlemen of the jury –

DMITRY: The Defence!

DEFENCE: My learned friend, in his hurtling troika, has ridden
rough-shod over the facts of this case. By all means let us
rein in the horses and examine these facts at the steady
pace of law. We are told money was missing; the prisoner
spent money; ergo, the prisoner is a thief. The prisoner was
in the garden; his father was murdered; ergo, the prisoner
is a parricide.

Gentlemen, this case demands more than rhetoric and
simple equations. In the pursuit of truth, we must search
for coincidence and prove what we find beyond a shadow
of doubt: that the prisoner received 3000 roubles from his

fiancee; that he paid two visits to Mokroye; that on the first occasion, he spent half this sum, retaining the other half in a purse which he hung round his neck; that he regarded this purse as a burden of guilt and released it at Mokroye on the night of the murder; that he spent no more that 700 that night and was found to have 800 on his person when arrested. Nowhere is it proved that he possessed more than this sum. Nowhere is it proved that he stole from his father. And nowhere, gentlemen, is it positively proved that his father had any money under his pillow to start with!

But his father was murdered. Who then, if not the prisoner, committed the crime? Was there anyone else in the garden that night? Who entered the house and left the door open? Even if we had no answer to these questions, we could only assume the prisoner's guilt by a process of elimination. The prisoner is the only suspect; ergo he did it.

But we *have* an answer, gentlemen of the jury: a formal confession and material proof, which I shall now lay before you.

On the night of the murder, in the servant's cottage, a few yards from the house, there lay, supposedly unconscious in his bed, a man widely rumoured to be the fourth son of Karamazov. This man made a statement to my principal witness, a gentleman of the highest integrity and intelligence who is known to you all. I call Ivan Karamazov.

IVAN: *(Coming forward.)* If I want to, I'll tell you; if I don't, I won't – like a little girl who will-you won't-you get up in the morning to me married. Would you like the money now? I have 3000 rainbows from behind the icon. Something very important which has a bearing on this case... So listen! A holy virgin was with child by the father, and her time was accomplished and she was delivered in the bath-house. And the child waxed strong and was a servant to the master, sat on his right hand and brewed his broth. Am I making myself clear? I told Smerdyakov that the fig-tree was barren and must be cut down! I closed my eyes and the train passed right over me. Here's my ticket.

I'm not continuing with the journey. Last night I was with him in the upper room, and he took a sock and dipped it in the blood and said to whomsoever I shall give this sock, that same shall betray me. And he cast down the 3000 pieces of silver and went away and hanged himself. I thirst. May I have some water please? What are you staring at? I killed my father. I watched two reptiles devour each other. You'd have done the same. You're doing it now! Man cannot live by bread alone: he must have circuses. But you want evidence. Of course. You shall have it. In due course. My witness has a cold, but he's here, I can feel it. He's under your chair! Get him! Get hold of him! He's slippery! Shut the door! Slam it on his tail! He will tell you on oath that I am not mad: just a murderer, walking the long road, a quadrillion kilometres, for two seconds of joy. Hosannah. *(Sinks down.)*

DMITRY: I am guilty of drunkenness and loose living. I am guilty of selfishness and greed. I am guilt of jealousy and thieving. I lived like a wild beast but I longed for goodness. You have found me guilty of killing my father. I did not kill him, I swear that before God. But I thank you for your verdict. I shall take my sword and break it over my head and kiss the pieces… *(Joins IVAN.)* I shall take my sword and break it over my head and kiss the pieces. I am guilty of drunkenness and loose living… *(Continues.)*

IVAN: I am not mad: just a murderer, walking the long road, a quadrillion kilometres, for two seconds of joy. Hosannah… I am not mad: just a murderer… *(Continues.)*

SMERDYAKOV: *(Joins them.)* I ended my life of my own free will and no one should be blamed for it. I ended my life of my own free will and no one should be blamed for it. I ended… *(Continues.)*

ALYOSHA: *(Out of the confusion.)* What is a father? He makes a child. In making a child, he acquires a duty: to love his child and let him grow. We are his children. In him we grew. In his love of life, in his passion, we grew. In his base desires, in his folly, we grew. In his envious lonely world, we grew, to be feared by him and to fear each other. He set us free to be slaves to our needs. He broke the sacred bond of brothers that redeems the hard work of man in the earth and feeds the hungry and builds peace for our sons. In anger we grew. In tears, constraint and rebellion, we grew: four brothers unknown to each other, bound by a common desire to avenge. The tyrant who breaks the back of his people must be killed by his people, and his people pay the price. We killed the seed that lived in us, and we share the guilt. We all share the guilt: one dead, one mad, one condemned – but not lost! If the earth is loved and watered with tears from its crust to its core, the dead seed lives. Let it take twenty years, the seed of Karamazov will grow to a tree and bear much fruit. We never die brothers. Remember we never die. Listen and join hands. Hear it swell in the ground and push up through the soil. Join hands all brothers, join hands from under the earth, and sing, let us sing: Hurrah for Karamazov!

*Slowly he rouses them and they rouse each other, hands joined, to sing – first one, then the others joining.*

BROTHERS: *(Sing.)*

– Joy divine adored immortal...
– Joy divine adored immortal...
– Joy divine adored immortal...
– Joy divine adored immortal
daughter of Elysium,
mad with rapture to the portal
of thy holy shrine we come!
Fashion's laws the world may sever
but thy magic joins again.
All mankind be brothers ever
'neath thy warm and gentle reign.

Joy divine adored immortal
daughter of Elysium,
mad with rapture to the portal
of thy holy shrine we come.
Fashion's laws the world may sever
but thy magic joins again.

All mankind be brothers ever
'neath thy warm and gentle reign.

From the brimming breast of nature
joy in fountains freely flows.
Just and unjust every creature
joy of bounteous nature knows.
Streams of wine and lovers' kisses
joyous laughing nature brings.
Bless'd by all who live she blesses
soaring high on angel wings,
soaring high on angel wings.

*THE END*

# VANITY

## A RESPONSE TO PUSHKIN'S
## EUGENE ONEGIN

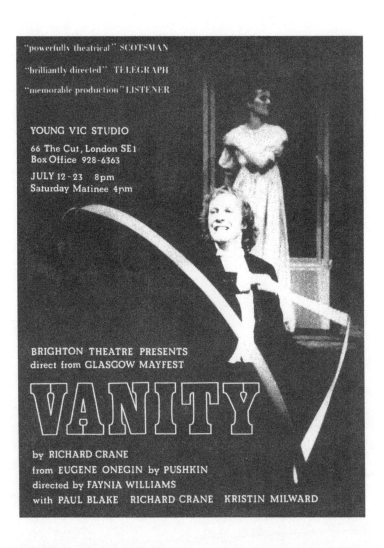

"powerfully theatrical" SCOTSMAN

"brilliantly directed" TELEGRAPH

"memorable production" LISTENER

YOUNG VIC STUDIO

66 The Cut, London SE1
Box Office 928-6363

JULY 12 - 23   8pm
Saturday Matinee 4pm

BRIGHTON THEATRE PRESENTS
direct from GLASGOW MAYFEST

# VANITY

by RICHARD CRANE
from EUGENE ONEGIN by PUSHKIN
directed by FAYNIA WILLIAMS
with PAUL BLAKE   RICHARD CRANE   KRISTIN MILWARD

# Characters

ONEGIN

TATYANA

LENSKY

*Vanity* was premiered by Brighton Theatre at the Pleasance, Edinburgh, 18th August 1980, where it won an Edinburgh Festival Fringe First Award.

*The cast was as follows:*

ONEGIN, Guy Manning
TATYANA, Nina Botting
LENSKY, Tom Bowles

*The play was directed and designed by* Faynia Williams.

*Vanity* was revived by Brighton Theatre at the Young Vic Theatre, London, 12th July 1983, with the following cast:

ONEGIN, Paul Blake
TATYANA, Kristin Milward
LENSKY, Richard Crane

*Directed and designed by* Faynia Williams.

# ONE

*ONEGIN and LENSKY play chess.*

LENSKY: How to open, let's consider:
    Cautiously, or brash and bold?
    Burst of glory, early death, or
    Living long and growing old?
    Some days I prefer the latter,
    Then the former seems the better;
    Always though the end's the same
    Because I never win the game!
    Not that I'm complaining, no!
    It is a privilege to lose
    To such a man as you sir, whose
    Acquaintance with a minor poet
    Such as me, is fair reward –

ONEGIN: Can we begin? I'm getting bored.

LENSKY: Fair enough! No more palaver!
    Silence rules the chequered floor.
    Come knight errant, mount your charger!
    Jump the pawns to Castle Four!

ONEGIN: Pawn to King Three.

LENSKY: Cautious, very.
    I could never be so wary.
    Being true romantic born,
    I lose patience with the pawn.
    No the knight's the piece I cherish,
    Ever noble, ever clean,
    In the service of his queen,
    Singing shrill and with a flourish:
    'Tirra lirra', to his love –

ONEGIN: Are you going to make your move?

LENSKY: Knight to Knight Five. Did I tell you – ?
    No you wouldn't understand.
    Your affairs are far too grand.
    Everyone has heard the stories,
    How you captivate the ladies,
    How they queue for you all day!

ONEGIN: What is it you're trying to say?

LENSKY: That I'm in love and she's a goddess:
    Ankles trim and waist so neat,
    And gentle mounds of bosom sweet
    Swelling up inside her bodice!
    By all the saints that ever were,
    I'd dare anything for her!

    Cross the Urals. Swim the Volga!
    I'm in love as ne'er before!
    Miles and miles I'd trudge for Olga!

ONEGIN: But she only lives next door.

LENSKY: You know her?

ONEGIN: No, I've never met her.

LENSKY: Swear you know no beauty better.

ONEGIN: If you like I'll swear the world
    Is flat and square with edges curled.

LENSKY: Elegiacs by the canto,
    Dithyrambs that know no end,
    All for Olga I have penned,
    And you may read them if you want to.
    It's so great to be alive!

ONEGIN: Queen to move to Castle Five.

LENSKY: That was dangerous. Did you mean it?
    Do you want to take it back?
    Foolish move if I may say so;
    Laid you open to attack.

> Check! You see, your pawn is taken,
> And your whole defence is shaken.

ONEGIN: King to Queen One.

LENSKY:  Onward fight,
> And storm the castle good Sir Knight!
> Look at that! Who can but wonder?
> Just one knight in just three moves,
> Checks the King beneath his hooves
> With pawn and castle knuckling under!
> Pure romance! Need I say more?

ONEGIN: Bishop move to Bishop Four.

LENSKY: Olga, did I mention Olga?

ONEGIN: Yes you did.

LENSKY:  Then may I now
> Risk the charge of overstatement
> And depict exactly how
> Lovely she is and quite delicious,
> Filling full my dearest wishes:
> Bright and bubbly, tender, true –

ONEGIN: And how does Olga feel for you?

LENSKY: She's delighted. She's devoted.
> Has been since the age of three:
> Childhood sweethearts, she and me,
> And a wedding has been mooted.
> But I wouldn't look so far,
> Take my blessings as they are!

> Marriage, middle-age and all
> That goes with family, hearth and home,
> Are considerations that
> A true romantic cannot own.
> Bliss of life in modest order,
> First a son and then a daughter,
> Fireside tales and cups of tea,

Dandling grandsons on my knee,
These are sweet, but want for action!
Burning love is all there is!
Taste the rapture of a kiss
And onward ride in one direction
Find success with victory capped!
So let's see where we are –

ONEGIN: You're trapped.

LENSKY: Oh. Yes. Well. Nil desperandum!
I've another knight to play,
Leap the line to Bishop Three
And drive the demon Queen away!
But I'm amazed, if I may say it,
At your game and how you play it,
For weren't you once, so rumour goes,
Quite the dizziest of beaux?
Every night engagements brimming
As from ball to ball you sped,
Scarcely ever saw your bed,
But sporting fashion's latest trimming,
Vaulted every stumbling-block
And whirled yourself around the clock!

People reeled as you flew higher
Challenging your luck to crack;
Lost a hundred, won a thousand,
Lost it all, then won it back –
Then lost it! Oh the social braying!

ONEGIN: Do you want to go on playing?

LENSKY: Sorry! Not another word!
I chatter like a mynah bird.
It is my one besetting weakness.
'Shut up please, and let it be!'
So Olga's always telling me,
With all her charm and lovely meekness.

You've not met her yet, have you?
She has an elder sister too.

It's your move. I'd protect the lady.
It's your turn. Are you awake?
Saints alive, I know I'm boring,
But this really takes the cake!
Yet again there's nothing sweeter
That the balm of rhyme and metre.

ONEGIN: Shall we finish?

LENSKY: It can wait.

ONEGIN: Queen takes Bishop's Pawn. Check mate.

LENSKY: That was brilliant. Quite astounding.
It's a privilege to yield
To one who clearly holds the field
And justifies his name resounding.
You are picked sir for success.
For chess is life, and life is chess.

# TWO

*TATYANA reading a book.*

TATYANA: Her hair was raven black, her face was white.
    Her lips were chapped as all alone she sat,
    Devouring lengthy novels through the night,
    And all around the snow was thick and flat.
    Her younger sister, nurse and mother lay
    Asleep and warm and sorting out their dreams,
    Of who to put with whom on Christmas Day,
    Of cherry jam and scones and custard creams.
    Alone, the icy wind across her face,
    Behind an ectoplasm of frosty breath,
    She read of heated lovers' close embrace,
    Of ecstasy, despair and sudden death!
    Alone and pale and older than her age,
    She licked a frozen thumb and turned the page.

    Dawn seeped across the sky, newborn and raw.
    A choir of busy early birds rehearsed.
    She sensed a new beginning was in store,
    Drank in the hope of spring and slaked her thirst.
    Her younger sister, nurse and mother rose
    And sorted out the order of the day:
    Which gown to wear, what shoes and underclothes,
    and how to keep the sister's beau at bay.
    For though the beau was suitably endowed
    And sanctioned by the motherly lorgnette,
    The pair were much too young to be allowed
    To contemplate the mooted marriage yet.
    Besides, and here's a factor must be faced:
    The elder sister was as yet unplaced.

    The beau arrived and smiling at his side,
    A certain dashing stranger, dark and tall.
    His neighbouring uncle recently had died,

And might he now presume to pay a call?
His voice was rich and light and advertised
A world of epigrams and subtle quips,
A mischief dancing in his flashing eyes,
A glint of invitation on his lips.
The beau and younger sister slipped away
To pet and cuddle out of sight and sound.
Would now the stranger go or would he stay?
He didn't seem, the type to wait around.
Excited by the way the novel led,
She skipped a page and this is what she read:

They thrashed and bit and grappled in the grass
With laughing tongues and teeth and tearing nails,
Devouring every minute as it passed
The juices of their bodies' holy grails:
The fullness of his lips, the seering scrape
Of shaven face against her milky skin,
The pain of bliss the screaming joy of *rape*
As lovely sweat and muscle plundered in!
He drove her to the chasm of the dead,
And almost on the edge, he stopped and grinned.
Then love exploded and her maidenhead
Was scattered black and bloody to the wind.
The dream disintegated as she lay.
The stranger was a million miled away.

# THREE

*ONEGIN and LENSKY on horseback.*

ONEGIN: Faster, he shouted, faster, faster!
    Race me, race, you dozy sheep!
    Give me a reason why I'm living!
    Wake me up; I'm fast asleep!

LENSKY: Could we go a little slower?
    We've been riding for a hour.
    What's the point in wearing out
    A horse I love and care about?

ONEGIN: What's the *point?* His words re-echoed
    Down the canyon of the night.
    The point is blunt and soft and trite!
    It's filed away, perfumed and lacquered.
    Race me race with all your might,
    To render it vital, keen and bright!

LENSKY: I'm quite prepared to be the whetstone
    On which you may hone your wits,
    But what confounded use can I be
    Frozen and shattered to bits?

ONEGIN: But you're a poet! Don't you feel
    A surging rush of molten steel
    Scalding through your icy cast
    The future flashing into past
    As present is struck out in lightning
    And you leap the vast abyss?
    Aren't you going through all this?
    Don't you feel the senses heightening?
    Cold? You can't be! Christ, it's hot!

LENSKY: I'm freezing like I don't know what.

ONEGIN: They cantered on a jumped a style

And neither had the wish to talk.
They trotted on for half a mile
And finally slowed to a walk.
The sky was black, the ground was white.
The moon and stars were out of sight.
The steaming, snorting horses filled
The silence, yawning, flat and chilled.

LENSKY: Steady boy...Phew! And thanks. I'm sorry
I do appreciate your need
For competition, dash and speed.
It's just that my need's not so keen
Since Olga beautified the scene.

ONEGIN: Olga?

LENSKY: Oh I know she's not your
Arch voluptuous *femme fatale* –

ONEGIN: Which one was Olga? I've forgotten.

LENSKY: The younger one, demure and small.

ONEGIN: She's dumb.

LENSKY: I think the word is 'meek'.

ONEGIN: No, dumb. I didn't hear her speak.

LENSKY: She keeps her sweet tongue in her head.

ONEGIN: And giggles and blinks and grins instead.

LENSKY: I don't know how to take this sir.

ONEGIN: Fight back at me.

LENSKY: That's not my style.

ONEGIN: Stand up to me! Demand a duel!

LENSKY: I wouldn't wish to go so far.
A sense of contest I agree,
Is admirable and ought to be

The force that regulates the way
Society ebbs and flows, but if

This force is carried out of hand
Becoming a matter of life and death,
The slender thread of give and take
Within society's web, will break.
Passion's contest must be checked
By humour, manners and respect.
Sorry, that sounded like a sermon!
Change the subject. What do you say?
Or let's be silent... By the way
Where are we?

ONEGIN: I don't know.

LENSKY: Come on,
You chose the route. Where are we going?
It's cold. It's very late. It's snowing.

ONEGIN: I haven't a clue.

LENSKY: But you were leading.

ONEGIN: Lost, we're lost.

LENSKY: Please don't provoke.
I thought you had the answer to
Everything. It's not a joke.

ONEGIN: My life's completely in your hands.

LENSKY: But I'm a poet; I don't make plans.

ONEGIN: So what's to do then?

LENSKY: Don't ask me!

ONEGIN: Lie down and die?

LENSKY: You led the way!
You raced ahead. I only wanted
To get home and go to bed.
I've got a busy day tomorrow.
I've got the inspectors coming round.
You don't appear to realize my
Character with Olga's family

Hangs by a thread. They place a low
Premium on romantic op-
Timism and knight errantry.
I've got to prove I'm capable
Of supporting their daughter
In the manner she's accustomed to.
I mean what are they going to say
When they find out I spent the night
Careering like a maniac
Half way around the world, crippling
My horse and dying of exposure?
I hope we *don't* survive. I hope
We're lost forever. I hope we
Freeze rigid and they dig us out
In fifty years: two skeletal
White knights who galloped off the board,
Nameless, bleached and horrible
Witnesses to the folly of
Challenging common sense.

ONEGIN: Do you see that light? There, straight ahead.
    And there's another. Do you see
    The way a third light comes in view,
    The shape in which the building rises?
    Have you seen this house before?
    Look, there's another light, and more.
    It seems your house is not asleep.
    They're waiting up for their lost sheep.

LENSKY: Incredible. I must be dreaming.
    I am struck completely mute.
    What a terrifying route!
    What audacious crafty scheming!

ONEGIN: It seemed to be the poet's intent
    To make a speech before he went.

LENSKY: Before we part, may I conjecture
    What it was conspired to send

You speeding hell-for-leather and firing
Vitriol at your closest friend?
For you have taught me the poet's duty,
To dig the earth for hope and beauty,
Even when it is choc-a-bloc
With rubble, rubbish, root and rock!
First it seems that you've been testing
How my love for Olga stands,
Whether it's built on shifting sands
Or firmly fixed and everlasting.
And we both have jointly proved
That never shall this love be moved!

Next it seems – are you still with me? –
Next a point, a sort of trend,
Which I would hesitate to mention
If you were not my closest friend.
It seems, you see, that you've been throwing
Caution to the winds and glowing
Ever since we both took tea
With Olga and her family.
Please tell me if I got it wrong,
But as I drank and ate my scone
I spotted something going on,
A look that lingered just too long…
The elder sister? Am I right?
Is that what sent you wild tonight?

No answer. Then I've hit it square,
And fortune on my fancy sits.
The four of us may join the dance.
The variegated pattern fits!
For though you may not be aware,
Society has you by the hair.
For many weeks it has been planned
That you should have the elder hand.
But you have turned a prim proposal

Back-to-front and upside-down!
The family walls have tumbled down.
The sisters are at our disposal!
And just what this means, I'll now
Elucidate if you'll allow…

ONEGIN: Dawn was near as he at last
Extended thanks and begged a pardon.
He'd been led around the world
And up the path of his own garden;
Had visited the vast abyss
That yawns for those that dare dismiss
The social laws of space and time,
Of manner, money, reason, rhyme.
So full of love and free from doubt,
Content and tired he went to bed,
His muses buzzing in his head,
As one by one the lights went out.
But on the features of his friend,
A much more deadly abyss grinned.

# FOUR

*TATYANA with a book.*

TATYANA: Nurse Nurse! The nurse rushed in: What is it dear? –
 I'm stifling. I can't breathe. I'm choking Nurse! –
 My my, she coughed. It's awful stuffy here,
 And flung the window wide. – No no! That's worse!
 I'm freezing! – Are you dear? She slammed it shut
 And felt her brow. – I'm cold. – You're not you know.
 You're feverish. You're brow is burning hot. –
 Don't leave me Nurse! Oh Nurse I love him so! –
 Love whom? – Oh Nurse I'm dying! Help me please! –
 Now pull yourself together. Be your age.
 She tucked her in and gave her wrist a squeeze:
 My poor poor baby child. You've torn the page
 Out of your book. We've got to get you strong.
 You really shouldn't read such stuff. It's wrong.

 Nurse, Nurse, when you were young, what was it like?
 Oh dear, I can't recall. Her face was red
 And shameful tears were smarting in her eyes. –
 Were you in love? – Oh heavens, never, no!
 She turned away. – Not once? Don't tell me lies.
 The Nurse said: Well just once, long long ago,
 But it's of no importance. – Yes, it *is*! –
 It's not a thing a girl should hear about. –
 That's why I want to hear it! Was it bliss,
 A joy you simply couldn't do without?
 How old were you? Were you as young as me?
 The Nurse surveyed the ceiling furiously.

 I might have been fourteen or maybe twelve,
 Thirteen or fifteen, definitely not more.
 I'm certain I was younger than yourself.
 How old I was exactly I'm not sure.
 My hair was in a pigtail down my back

And I had freckles all across my face.
I had to clean the hearth; my hands were black,
And all my fingernails were a disgrace!
He was a soldier staying at the house.
I never knew his rank or who he was.
I always kept as silent as a mouse;
I never was a one to make a fuss.
He left the house the night I was defiled
And he was killed. He never saw his child.

Oh Nurse that's sad, so sad! – And now my dear,
It's time to go to sleep. She smoothed the bed:
I've chattered on for far too long I fear.
She tucked her up and kissed her on the head. –
But aren't you angry? Suddenly the girl
Sat up and cried: To think that you and he
Could never shout it out to the whole world
That you were so in love, it *had* to be! –
I never use that word and nor should you.
It's dangerous, it's evil and it's wrong. –
But *I'm* in love! I *am*! – That is not true.
The Nurse's voice was temperate and strong:
You're sick, it's late, you're very tired indeed.
A good night's gentle sleep is what you need.

I need some paper and a pen and ink.
I'm not a child. You will do as I say.
The little Nurse's face was prim and pink. –
Quick, hurry! And she left in disarray.
Presently she returned. The girl was seated
Silent at the table, took the pen
And ink and paper, murmuring a flat
Good Night. The Nurse went tiptoe out again.
The candle flamed and leapt and licked the wax
And flicked satanic shadows on the walls.
The rapid pen pursued its serried tracks,
And filled the paper, never stopped at all.

She poured her very heart into the note,
And this is just a part of what she wrote.

# FIVE

*TATYANA writing/ONEGIN reading a letter.*

TATYANA: I know it's not a lady's place
    To write to a gentleman like this.
    I know it's not a lady's place
    To write to a gentleman at all!
    She must wait and fret and panic,
    Bite her nails and take a tonic,
    Sit and groan, and weep and sigh
    And chip the heavy hours away.
    Well I've waited and I've fretted,
    Panicked, groaned and wept and sighed
    And every night lain wide awake
    For two months. Ever since your visit
    I've been hammering my head
    Against a granite prison bed.

    Why did you come? If you had stayed
    Away, my life would have gone on,
    Dull and bleak but bearable
    Because I wouldn't need to hope.
    I wouldn't know what I was missing.
    I'd continue fantasizing,
    Bathing in romantic streams
    Of novels, magazines and dreams;
    While my family packaged me
    Into an early womanhood,
    And led to market dumb and good
    I'd be exhibited, and my teeth,
    Hair, skin, eyes, height, weight, shape, size
    Intelligence and disposition,
    Special peculiarities,
    Pedigree and breeding stock
    Would all be fully scrutinized

And maybe I'd secure a mate
Of suitably highborn estate,
Of middle or advancing years,
Who'd lead me down the aisle in tears,
Invade my body with a grunt
And put himself out to grass when he
Had sired sufficient family,
And I'd continue quite content
With daily chores and social calls,
Good works and mothercraft and balls.

TATYANA/ONEGIN: That's not the life for me. That's why
    I'm writing to you. Can't you see
    That you and I, were meant to be.

ONEGIN: *(Reading)* A long time ago, before you ever
    Actually came to see us,
    I dreamed about you and I knew
    Your face, your voice, your manner, how
    You entered a room and how you smiled
    And how you stood and how you sat
    And yawned at superficial chat
    And fidgetted like an angry child.
    Everything was in the dream.
    I even knew your name.

    And every dream was one step closer.
    First we were tongue-tied and gauche,
    Then we found a sense of humour,
    Then by accident we touched,
    And kissed and found we were
    Tongue-tied again…
    But since you came to see us, since
    You entered the room and smiled and sat
    And yawned and went, those dreams have gone
    And I lie in bed terrified it's all
    A plot to send me mad.

    I'm not going to read this letter through.

I'll seal it, send it, let it come
Flapping through your letter-box for you
To stack on the pile of all the other dumb
And reckless rubbish you receive each week
From girls who are too sick with love to speak.
You can do as you like, it's up to you.
I've laid my bleeding heart bare on a plate.
You can ignore it or tear it in two
Or pity or mock its poor pathetic state…

TATYANA: Or alternatively you might
Mount your fiery charger white
And gallop through the howling night
And hear my choked and feeble call
And scale the granite castle wall
And break the iron chain and ball
And then – Oh ecstasy of bliss! –
Embrace and wake me with a kiss!

# SIX

*Maytime in the country.*

LENSKY: It's May, and trees are frilled with blossom.
　　Ewes are suckling baby lambs.
　　Aunts and mothers, proud of bosom
　　Serve with cream their scones and jams.
　　Sap is rising, buds are bursting,
　　Laughing lips prepare for feasting.
　　Gardens buzz with idle chat
　　Of such and such and this and that:
　　Of pretty Olga and her mooted
　　Husband: when will they be wed?
　　The day cannot be far ahead.
　　But first her sister must be suited.
　　Olga lingers in the shade
　　Till someone wed the older maid.

　　Who will it be? Will it be he
　　Who paid a visit months ago? –
　　And never since has graced the scene?
　　One surely can't imagine so! –
　　But who else is there? She's so moody,
　　Secretive and quite contrary.
　　As long as she denies herself,
　　Her sister wilts upon the shelf. –
　　But who is this? A horseman racing
　　Down the drive toward the house!
　　Could it be he, the would-be spouse?
　　Does anyone know his social placing?
　　Is it the stranger? – Yes! The same! –
　　Does anybody know his name?

TATYANA: She bolted out of the house across the lawn
　　And leapt the ha-ha, tangling in the scrub,
　　And smarting nettle-stung and bramble-torn,
　　Raced across the paddock, jumping shrub

And hillock, gorse and grassy bank,
And losing a shoe, she blundered through a brake,
And slipped, got up and slithered, till she sank
Down on a broken bench beside the lake.

ONEGIN: He slipped out of the house and strode across
The lawn, then cleared the ha-ha, to take
The paddock with its hillocks and its gorse
At a steady pace until he found the lake.

TATYANA: The sun was overhead, the sky was blue.
He stopped and smiled and handed her a shoe.

ONEGIN: I read your letter. He expected her
To laugh and throw herself into his arms
Or jump for joy and dive into the lake,
Or just look up and blind him with her eyes.

I didn't know you felt so strongly.
I never received a letter
So open and honest.
I see it therefore as my duty
To match your openness with mine
And answer you straight down the line.

His words were hollow. All too pat they came
And bounced off her convulsing little frame.

If I were sure I could be happy
Living a sweet domestic life
With all the hopes and fears and blessings
Of children, home and darling wife;
If I were sure this were my pattern,
Then all my doubts would be forgotten,
For I would look to you alone
To share my family and my home.

He wanted her to break his flow of speech,
But she was huddled up and out of reach.

This also is my own conclusion

That such a life is not for me,
Though in my case a variation
In  reasoning exists. You see
I do admire the faith and courage
That work to make a blissful marriage
And I would dearly love to share
The griefs and joys that mingle there.
But much too well do I know my nature.
I'm restless, always shall be so.
I never arrive, but I must go.
I'd lead any wife a life of torture.
We'd never laugh and seldom speak.
I'd hate it after a single week.

He tossed a stone and watched the ripples break
His elegant reflection in the lake.

So there are two reason why I shouldn't
Appeal to me if I were you:
The first that I, though fine in theory,
In practical terms, just would not do;
And secondly, it comes over clearly,
That though we feel for each other dearly,
The basic views we hold at heart,
Are diametrically, far apart.
I like marriage and you hate it.
You could suffer it; I could not.
There lies, I feel, the seed of rot.
It would be folly to progagate it.
But may this difference never seep through
To the brotherly love I feel for you.

So would you therefore object, if I
Presumed to offer once or twice
A piece that is sincerely meant
Of loving brotherly advice?
For though you may not now believe it,
Your heart is yours and you'll retrieve it,

Free and proud to love again,
The cream of eligible men.
Please then observe this minor warning:
Don't be as open as you've been
With me, for it may not be seen
As fitting a young lady's bearing.
I understood, but you may find
That others are not quite so kind.

TATYANA: The sun went in.
The sky was grey.
He seemed to have
No more to say.
The wind was sharp.
He seemed to yawn
As they returned
Across the lawn.

# SEVEN

*June to October.*

LENSKY: June! Hot summer! Tongues are flapping.
    Lungs inflate for madrigal.
    Gossip trills in high soprano.
    Scandal fills the alto role. –
    Will they wed and weave together
    Bliss of love and pleasant weather? –
    Never! He is far too fast!
    Do you know nothing of his past? –
    But it's the future she is seeking.
    How she longs for him to say;
    With this ring I name the day!
    How her darling heart is aching! –
    Let her fling the cupboard wide
    Wherein his flighty habits hide!

ONEGIN: Seven o'clock, his valet gently coughs,
    To wake him and present his dressing-gown.
    He executes the first yawn of the day
    And steps into the gown and leaping down
    The stairs, three at a time, he is away,
    Across the yard and down the rutted track,
    Straight through a busy poultry conference
    Which scatters with a cock-a-doodle-quack,
    As down to the river he runs, and leaps the fence
    And flings aside the gown and splashes in,
    And swims across and back and splashes out
    And runs back to the hall where with a grin
    His healthy breathing meets the ancient wheeze
    Of housekeeper bringing his coffee and cheese.

TATYANA: She can't sleep. She lies blind
    Staring ahead. She can't find
    Her way through the pitch night.
    She's thin, old and deathly white.

She dreams with her eyes wide
And shuts the summer outside
And walks across the snowy plane
Of cold soft counterpane.
A thick, black, misty gloom
Permeates the huge room.
Suddenly she stops short.
A river roars in full flood:
A boiling billowing main,
Frothing red like blood.
She daren't sweat, she can't shiver.
A stick bridge spans the river.

LENSKY: July! And now the kith and kindred
Transpose to a major key
Their tightly laced and crisply laundered
Counterpoint and harmony. –
Soon we'll know the great decision.
Soon our hopes will find fruition.
He's simply playing hard to get.
We'll call his bluff and win him yet! –
Maybe we will, and maybe presently
She'll have cause to weep for shame.
It can't be he'll forsake the game
He's played so long and so intently –
Haven't you heard? His past is sunk.
He lives as pure as a sainted monk!

ONEGIN: Breakfast over, he proceeds to dress
In sober greens and browns. His tailor calls
And measures him for slacks and modish tweeds.
The silk embroidered suit to wear at balls
Is cancelled. He has countrified his needs.
Eleven o'clock, he's seated at his desk,
Thumbs through accounts and files the morning mail,
Like any clerk, perfunctory and brief.
That done, he skims a magazine, until

His horse is ready saddled at five to ten.
He canters here and there on business calls
To overseers, tenants and the men
And women of the lowest social groove
Whose lot in life he's working to improve.

TATYANA: She dares not cross the bridge.
Behind her a snowy ridge,
Rises, breaks and there
Rears a roaring bear!
She scuttles with a tight scream
Over the red-hot stream.
The bear leaps across, comes
Lumbering as she runs,
Knee-deep, very slow
Through thick driven snow.
She can't win, but must try,
Blunders into a pine wood,
Slapped and kicked by
Vicious trees. Should
She heave on or fall down?
She trips and plunges to the ground.

LENSKY: August! Now the song is longer,
Hotter, lazier, but still
Confident in speculation
Of what won't or might or will
Become of Olga and her sister
And their future lords and masters.

ONEGIN: After lunch, he reads or walks or rides.
He can't be still; he mustn't ease the pace
Or stop to wonder what he's living for,
Or let too many yawns invade his face.
Sometimes a book from his extensive store
Will keep him occupied for half an hour,
Provided it is fairly frivolous.
And if it rains, he'll maybe brave the shower,

Galloping till he's sodden to the skin
And forced to find a nameless peasant wife
With dancing eyes and a nervous grin,
Who'll take him in and gently dry his clothes
And warm him in the only way she knows.

TATYANA: The bear stops, raises her,
Hugs her in warm fur,
Carries her through the trees
To a clearing where she sees
A cottage. Light shines
Behind the pretty window blinds.
The bear nudges open the door
And drops her gently on the floor.
She sits alone in a hall.
Another door, rather small,
Emits a soft, warm, dull
Buzz of guests in party mood,
The murmuring of mouths full
Of conversation and food.
Eager to find out more,
She puts her eye to a crack in the door.

LENSKY: September. Things are getting serious.
Olga and her beau can't wait. –
I'm afraid they'll have to wait.
Her sister first must find a mate. –
She *has* a mate. She *is* intended. –
That affair has long since ended.

ONEGIN: At home again, it's only half past three.
He sets the billiard table, takes a cue,
And silently perfects the perfect game,
And chalks away a lengthy hour or two,
While family ghosts from every picture frame
Remind him he's the last one of the line.
He often wonders why he's living here,
And how he came and what he left behind,

The day his debts pursued him to the bed
Of his rich uncle, who when he arrived,
Was kind enough to be already dead.
He pots the red and pads about the room,
A stranger playing billiards in a tomb.

LENSKY: October. Quavers turn to crotchets.
Minims turn to semi-breves.
Olga whiles away the hours
Trying to catch the falling leaves.
Indoors the gossips rasp and jar
Around the eternal samovar.

TATYANA: She gasps aloud at what she sees.
Her skin crawls, her veins freeze.
The room slurps, cackles, shrieks,
With hell's melee of monster-freaks!
Bulbous humps of bland skin –
She knows them all – her kith and kin!
Her mother with three heads devours
Her baby niece. Her uncle cowers,
Legless, armless on the floor,
Sipping vomit through a straw.
Her bald and withered grandma lies
Giving birth to giant slugs
From every pulsing orifice
With urine steaming from her dugs.
And over all presides supreme
The yawning stranger of her dream.

He flings the door wide.
She's there. – Come inside. –
She's ours, say hungry kith and kin:
We've laid a place for you. Come in.
Her aunt is retching blood and phlegm.
He laughs: Take no account of them.
They vanish. Alone now, he sinks
His head upon her lap. She thinks:

This must be heaven, but then
Olga giggling and her poet come in.
The stranger leaps up. She sees the gleam
Of a knife! The poet's down. Her body wild
Is bolted upright on a scream!
No! No! No! No! No!
No… No… My baby child…
The Nurse is sitting by the bed,
With a damp flannel, dabbing her head.

ONEGIN: The summer's past. What progress has been made
In his campaign to wish to stay alive?
How long can he go on just 'going on'?
Each day is built with heavy measured blocks,
Whose purpose is to circumscribe the void,
And fortify the ticking of the clocks.
His neighbour poet's coming round at nine
To decorate the boredom with his chat
And soak the evening hours in pleasant wine:
A man of little sparkle or suspense,
But anything is better than silence.

# EIGHT

*ONEGIN and LENSKY at dinner.*

LENSKY: Do you remember Olga's sister?
    It's her name-day in a week.
    They're having a celebration
    And they've asked me to speak
    To you to see if you'll be coming.
    Should be quite a jolly evening.

ONEGIN: He asked him if the gathering would be
    The usual society jamboree.

LENSKY: No, not at all. It's very small.
    A smattering of family friends;
    No pandering to current trends.
    Honest amusement is the rule.
    Round games and games of cards,
    Formation dancing and charades.

ONEGIN: It sounded awful: just the sort of show
    He'd given up attending long ago.

LENSKY: I really ought to give *you* up.
    I don't know why I work so hard.
    I'd sooner try to milk a duck,
    Or entertain a slab of lard.
    I don't believe that you were picked
    To be a social derelict.
    You're not by nature misanthropic,
    And though you're prickly on the topic,
    I am going to say it straight:
    Net your fish before a school
    Of hungry sharks invade the pool.
    And do it quick; it's not too late.
    She thinks your charming, fond and clever.
    But she won't think that way for ever.

ONEGIN: He laughed it off and let the subject go
    Without  giving a definite yes or no.

# NINE

*The Name-Day Ball.*

TAYANA: *(Before her mirror.)*
> The image sat before her staring back.
> You're hard as marble, cold as ice, she said.
> Your hair is stiff like neatly matted rope.
> Your eyes are like ball-bearings in your head.
> Why rouge your cheeks pretending you're a tart?
> Your lips have never kissed. Why paint them red?
> Your pearls are like a noose around your neck.
> You're hard and hollow, frigid, false and dead.
>
> The image answered back: From where I sit,
> It's possible to see your features too.
> Your eyes are red and ringed. You face is lined.
> Your cheeks are sunk. Your lips are taut and blue.
> Your nerves are shreds. Your breasts have disappeared.
> Your old and sick. Your bones are poking through.
> You wouldn't last one moment at the ball.
> It's just as well *I'm* going and not *you*.

LENSKY: In the hall the guests were trading
> Bows and kisses, hugs and shrieks. –
> Hello, how wonderful to see you!
> Where've you been? It must be weeks! –
> May I introduce my daughter?
> How's your mother? Have you brought her? –
> Where's your sister Olga dear?
> Don't tell me she isn't here!

TATYANA: The image was conveyed into the hall
> And parked upon a dais to perform
> Her greetings to the guests as they approached,
> Singly, severally or in a swarm.

LENSKY: Isn't she ravishing? What beauty,
> Dignity and glowing poise!

How she stuns the popinjays
And captivates the bully-boys!

TATYANA: The witty cliches and the glib retorts
Came tripping off her tongue obediently
And she was decked about with compliments,
Like twinkling baubles on a Christmas tree.

LENSKY: I can't believe she's not as yet
Matched up and fully spoken for;
But she'll be stepping out you bet
Before the morning, that's for sure!

TATYANA: She almost was beginning to enjoy
The roars of laughter and the generous fun.
The wine was slowly warming up her blood.
The thaw it seemed had finally begun.

ONEGIN: He enters breathless, flinging off his cloak
And bows to Olga's mother, kisses hands,
Begs pardon for being late and laughs
And everyone laughs back and understands.

LENSKY: The buzz subsides as he comes in,
And spectacles, lorgnettes and eyes
Aim their sights in his direction:
What an interesting surprise!
Does he have the gall to court her,
Asks the world his wife and daughter,
After so disgracefully
Neglecting her? It cannot be!

TATYANA: He sees her and her heart forgets to beat.
The floor is swept away beneath her feet.
What mad intent made him come here today?
He's coming towards her smiling all the way.

ONEGIN: The ball is larger than he was told.
This angers him and leaves him cold.
The painted lady in her cage
Further exacerbates his rage.

TATYANA: We're honoured sir that you are pleased
    To attend our celebration.

ONEGIN: The greater honour's mine mam'selle
    To extend congratulation.

TATYANA: We trust you will enjoy the food
    And wine and pleasant company.

ONEGIN: I promise you I shall enjoy
    The evening unreservedly.

LENSKY: Then with the sound of popping corks,
    The guests' attention quickly strays,
    With happy squeaks and hungry squawks,
    To a procession of trays,
    Which discharge their burden of champagne,
    Retreat and then return again,
    Sailing through the frothing mass,
    Majestic and mountainous,
    With food of every breadth and height:
    Stout hams and bloated pies – a swan!
    A sucking pig – its head still on!
    The guests are shrieking with delight.

ONEGIN: The guests guffaw and stuff themselves with dips,
    And pate, borsch and kraut and quiche lorraine,
    And then with blurts and gulps and smacking lips
    They hack the pig to pieces and begin
    To disembowel the swan and wrench its wings.

TATYANA: She stands apart
    With heaving heart
    As hard as marble
    Cold as ice,
    Coiffed and rinsed,
    Perfumed and lacquered,
    Next in line
    For sacrifice.

LENSKY: A toast!

ONEGIN: The poet leaps upon
    A chair.

LENSKY: Attention everyone
    And hear this verse!

ONEGIN: The guests complain
    And are placated with champagne.

LENSKY: Ode to a Name Day! Please suspend
    Applause and laughter till the end.

TATYANA: If I stand still and hardly breathe, perhaps
    The image will hold out and not collapse.

LENSKY: Crisp and golden hung the morning.
    Harvest fruits were gathered in,
    Russet leaves the earth adorning,
    Winter straining to begin,
    As a stork from heaven winging,
    From its beak a bundle swinging,
    Soared and swooped and with a whoosh,
    Dived into a gooseberry bush!
    So she was born and heaven's bounty
    Sent a virgin saint to bless
    The child with grace and gentleness,
    And lend her halo, name and beauty.
    So raise your glasses of champagne
    With me to toast the sainted name!

TATYANA: They raise their glasses to this show of wit.
    The mask is smiling wide enough to split.

LENSKY: A second verse, your kind attention!
    Hear how beautifully the child
    Grew with heavenly contradiction:
    Warmly cool, serenely wild!
    And how she had a younger sister –
    Over there in case you missed her –
    Fancy-free with golden hair,
    Delectable beyond compare!

I say this with a tinge of bias,
For it's to her mellifluous tune
That I will sing my verse as soon
As wedding-bells may sanctify us.
So while we have a glass in hand,
For Olga may I bid you stand!

ONEGIN: Olga unrehearsed in all this fun,
Raises her glass and downs it all in one.

LENSKY: And finally, just one more stanza,
Then it's onward with the ball.
May I direct your kind attention
To what I presume to call
The latent purpose of this evening,
Why it's bright and so enlivening,
Why this lady on my right,
Is looking so radiant tonight!
For she has found this evening handy
For setting her most attractive cap
At a certain dashing chap –
And it fits him fine and dandy!
So for these two I beg you drain
Your bubbling glasses once again!

TATYANA: The tears were welling up behind the mask.
To die, and instantly, is all I ask.

ONEGIN: What do I do? Leave or stay?
Stick it out or slip away?
If I stay, the choices are
sterile peace or open war.
I can love, *in my own time*,
Won't be forced or kept in line.
Fearful virgin dressed as whore
Is not what I bargained for.

Across the room, neglected Olga drinks.
Her poet's handing food around and thinks

She'll wait for him, but she's a little minx.
I watch her and she watches me, and winks.

LENSKY: *Voulez-vous un vol-au-vent?*
Which dip are you after: pink or blue?
Do grab some flan before it's gone,
And take a breast of chicken too.

TATYANA: My bones stick out. My breasts have disappeared.
My cheeks are sunk. My eyes are ringed and red.
The plaster image has quit, just as I feared.
The party guests are left with me instead.

LENSKY: Music! The waltz! Let's clear the floor!
The guests are chirping: wouldn't it be
Just fabulous if he and she
Were partnered! What are they waiting for?

ONEGIN: The poet moves to Olga. So do I.
I beat him to it and I sign her on.
She hands her glass to him and off we fly,
The first across the floor, and everyone
Scatters and clucks like bantam hens and cocks,
As tender chicken whirls with Mr Fox!

TATYANA: The poet pushes through the milling mass,
To sign me for his partner I suppose,
Seeing it as his duty to transform
A wilting wallflower into a rose.

ONEGIN: She's light and bright.
She weighs a feather.
Round and round
We fly together,
Spinning this way
Then the other,
To the amazement
Of her mother,
Aunts and uncles,
Cousins, nieces,

Tearing tastefulness
To pieces!

LENSKY: What a wonderful night.
You must be so proud.
Such a marvellous
And enlivening crowd.
You do look radiant tonight.
Is everything
All right...?

ONEGIN: Warm and firm
The music grips
Her body to me
And her lips,
Slightly parted
Full and red,
Signal a wish
To go ahead
Beyond the dance
To further sport
Whether or not
We really ought...

TATYANA: The dance went on for hours. When it stopped,
He led me to my seat, politely dropped
Me like a bag of bones and smiled his way
Through the perspiring, pink and puffing melee,
To where his Olga sat, no longer meek,
But roaring like a furnace, couldn't speak,
Just laughed and heaved and sweated like a worker.

LENSKY: Your hand is mine my love, for the Mazurka.

ONEGIN: Mazurka! She fell off her seat!
I couldn't! Think of my poor feet!
She threw herself back on her chair,
And laughing, tried to primp her hair.
I'm such a mess! I couldn't dance

Another step! No earthly chance!
I'm sorry, and don't look so cross.
She grinned and downed another glass.

LENSKY: The Mazurka is a dance I've always hated.
It fuels the brutish instinct of the crowd.
Its entertainment value's over-rated.
It's violent, common, coarse and much too loud.

TATYANA: Bam-ba-bam-bam! Bam-bam-bam!

ONEGIN: Come on Olga! On your feet!
It's the Mazurka! *Vite! Vite!*

TATYANA: Bam-ba-bam-bam! Bam-bam-bam!

LENSKY: Of course I don't mind! She's having fun.
I'm happy, flattered! I really am,
That she's so free with everyone.
I honestly don't give a damn!

TATYANA: Bam-ba-bam-bam! Bam-bam-bam!

ONEGIN: *Holupiec* and *pas marche*!
Damn tomorrow, live today!

TATYANA: Bam-ba-bam-bam! Bam-bam-bam!

LENSKY: I'm delighted she's with my friend.
It's great! It's absolutely fine,
Because you see I know in the end
She is indisputably *mine*.

TATYANA: Bam-ba-bam-bam! Bam-bam-bam!

ONEGIN: *Pas mazur* and circle me,
*Coup de talon!* Love is free!

TATYANA: Bam-ba-bam-bam! Bam-bam-bam!

LENSKY: I might have things to say to her
As any future husband might,
But that's entirely my affair.
It's down to me to put it right.

TATYANA: Bam-ba-bam-bam! Bam-bam-bam!

ONEGIN: *Chasse chasse* across the floor!
    Olga Olga! *Je t'adore!*

TATYANA: Bam-ba-bam-bam! Bam-bam-bam!

LENSKY: I know my duty, when to stop her
    When to step in and stop him too,
    If their behaviour seems improper.
    Believe me, I know what to do!

TATYANA: Bam-ba-bam-bam! Bam-bam-bam!

ONEGIN: Olga's lips were made to kiss…
    Closer, bam-ba-bam, like this…

TATYANA: Bam-ba-bam-bam! Bam-bam-bam…

LENSKY: I know when things have gone too far,
    And when to say: Right! That's enough!
    I know what decent standards are
    And once I'm roused, by God I'm tough!

ONEGIN: I don't know what you're on about.

LENSKY: You've taken my financee sir
    And led her in a drunken rout
    And made a spectacle of her.

ONEGIN: The only spectacle I see
    Is glaring straight ahead of me.

LENSKY: I freely grant your dancing is
    Performed with rare alacrity,
    And while I don't begrudge a kiss
    Within the laws of chivalry,
    I have to ask you now to aim
    At one who has a prior claim.

    You've partnered Olga every dance.
    Her sister is beside herself.
    You've spat upon the word romance
    And grievously impaired her health.

ONEGIN: Women who weep and have a fad
    For nervous breakdowns, drive me mad.

LENSKY: But this is more than madness sir,
    Deliberately to provoke
    Public disgrace and downright
    Despair as if it were a joke!
    I don't know what has brought this on
    Or where your courtesy has gone.

    I did presume you were my friend –

ONEGIN: All right, all right, you've said enough –

LENSKY: But honour sir, I must defend.

ONEGIN: Is this a challenge or a bluff?
    I need to know.

LENSKY: Don't force me sir.

ONEGIN: Stand up to me.

LENSKY: It's premature
    To stake our friendship –

ONEGIN:  Don't retreat!

LENSKY: If you will grant me Olga's hand…

ONEGIN: You mean I keep her legs and feet?

LENSKY: You've forced a challenge. I demand
    Satisfaction. Please expect
    A note tomorrow to that effect.

TATYANA: Bam-ba-bam-bam! Bam-bam-bam!

ONEGIN: Holupiec and pas marche!
    Damn tomorrow, live today!

TATYANA: Bam-ba-bam-bam! Bam-bam-bam!

ONEGIN: *Pas mazur* and circle me,
    *Coup de talon!* Love is free!

TATYANA: Bam-ba-bam-bam! Bam-bam-bam!

ONEGIN: Bam-ba-bam-bam! Bam-bam-bam!

TATYANA: The dancers yelled and juddered round the floor.
   The night was getting heavy, dull and slow.
   They didn't know what they were doing it for,
   And two by two they went back to gateaux,
   Meringue, blancmange, parfait, trifle and mousse,
   Not knowing why they wanted that either,
   Till gradually they started to disperse.
   The weary band played on not knowing who for.
   The aunts and mothers waded through the mess.
   God bless, good night, sleep very tight, they said,
   And Olga retched and vomited down her dress,
   And someone had to cart her up to bed.
   And I was left alone on my Name Day.
   The stranger was a million miles away.

# TEN

*The Duel.*

LENSKY: I sent the letter.

ONEGIN: In the morning
   A neighbour named Zaretsky called

LENSKY: Tomorrow sunrise –

ONEGIN: said the letter.

LENSKY: By the ruined watermill.

ONEGIN: He waited for an answer from me –

LENSKY: I checked the pistols carefully.

ONEGIN: Which I gave him short and firm.

LENSKY: I won't be seeing Olga –

ONEGIN: Then
   I swam , had breakfast, dressed –

LENSKY: I mustn't
   Think of her.

ONEGIN: Read through the post.

LENSKY: What time is it?

ONEGIN: Mustn't watch
   The clock.

LENSKY: She will be dressing now –
   Having breakfast, taking a walk –

ONEGIN: What brought this on?

LENSKY: – and weeping for me.

ONEGIN: Anger? Never felt it in
   My life. Principle? Never had
   Any. Necessity? Never believed
   In it. Boredom? Want of anything
   Better to do…?

LENSKY: I saddled my horse and galloped round
　　To see her. She was sewing a doll,
　　A little pale but not distressed.
　　She jumped up, threw her arms round me
　　And laughed! Didn't remember a thing
　　About last night except that I
　　Left early.

ONEGIN: If apathy is
　　The reason, why bother?

LENSKY: I kissed
　　Her and we played a game
　　And then I left.

ONEGIN: We'll call it off.

LENSKY: We'll call it off! I'm glad to be alive!

ONEGIN: I had some lunch.

LENSKY: I had some lunch.
　　Lentil broth, beef, potatoes, turnips
　　And lardy-cake with a thick sauce.

ONEGIN: Just an egg. It was fertilized.
　　I ate it raw.

LENSKY: I browsed a bit

ONEGIN: I tried to read.

LENSKY: I wrote a poem,
　　Not my best.

ONEGIN: I fell asleep.

LENSKY: I leapt up! Honour! What is it?
　　A fleeting vagary? A whim
　　To be shrugged off? Another word
　　For pique?

ONEGIN: Languor, is it
　　Curable?

LENSKY: Or is it a fact of life?
  An *a priori* truth, the rock
  On which society is built,
  The bond of love without which love
  Is cheap, the sword of sanity,
  The legend on the Holy Grail?

ONEGIN: I dragged myself awake.

LENSKY: I cleaned
  And polished the pistols.

ONEGIN: Played some billiards.

LENSKY: The custom is to take an aim
  For thigh or brain depending on
  How serious the argument.
  This argument is serious,
  So serious, it cannot be
  Dismissed by a direct hit to
  The brain. Some good must come of it.
  The lesson must be learnt. I shall
  Aim for the thigh.

ONEGIN: A direct hit
  And straight into the pocket.

LENSKY: Whether
  I hit or not is another matter.
  The point will have been made.

ONEGIN: I fell
  Asleep and dimly recollect
  Observing through a pane of glass
  My valet and my housekeeper,
  Whispering, worried what to do.
  They walked around the crystal cage
  And tapped it with a billiard cue.

LENSKY: But what if he should aim at me –

ONEGIN: They put their shoulders to the glass –

LENSKY: And hit the brain?

ONEGIN:– and gingerly
　　Heaved me up the stairs to bed.

LENSKY: I woke at five shivering.
　　The bedclothes had fallen off.
　　My left leg was still asleep.
　　Must have been the way I was lying.
　　I leapt up, ran on the spot,
　　Opened the window, just a notch.
　　A bitter wind was whistling in the dark.
　　I shut it and washed and shaved and dressed
　　Made a cup of coffee
　　And sat by the door listening.
　　The wind had dropped.
　　A distant dog.
　　The clock.
　　A knock. I let Zaretsky in.
　　He didn't speak. I got my coat.
　　He took the pistols, checked them, shut
　　The box. I followed him outside
　　And closed the door.

ONEGIN: The glass was clouded. Neighbour poet
　　And Olga's sister, lathered, scrubbed
　　To get it clean. They couldn't hear me
　　Shouting that the film of grime
　　Was on the inside. I hammered
　　And screamed against the glass,
　　Merely confirming their advice
　　That I should never be released.

LENSKY: It's half-past seven.

ONEGIN: I broke the glass
　　And shot downstairs, tearing into
　　Trousers, shirt and boots and coat,
　　The valet tumbling after me.

LENSKY: He's late.

ONEGIN: I flung the stable open.
    Fix the bridle! Leave the saddle!
    Where are you off to sir? – Leap up
    In front and hurry man! Come on!

LENSKY: The honour's mine if he does not
    Appear.

ONEGIN: We shot through the night.
    I gripped the little valet tight.
    The rosy fingers of the dawn
    Were inching into the sky! Come on!

LENSKY: It's dawn. He's obviously not coming.
    We'll give him another five minutes.

ONEGIN: We thundered into the village.
    It was beginning to stir.
    Some women were laughing
    With buckets for milking.
    A blacksmith was singing.
    We had to slow down to let some cattle pass.
    The valet was numb with anger
    That he'd ever woken me.
    We ran over a child and shot out of the village.

LENSKY: We'd better be getting home.

ONEGIN: The watermill rose in the pale light.
    Two stick figures stood by the stream.
    They saw us. They didn't move.
    We slowed to a trot as they grew nearer.
    Their faces were pinched.
    Good morning! Sorry we're late!
    We dismounted.

LENSKY: We walked beyond the mill
    No one spoke.
    Pistols were loaded,

Cloaks removed.
Zaretsky measured thirty-two paces.
We stood on our marks.

ONEGIN: March!

LENSKY: Where to aim? Brain or thigh?

ONEGIN: Earth... Feet...

LENSKY: Kill, maim, be maimed, or die?

ONEGIN: Frost... Face...

LENSKY: Who rules? Free will or fate?

ONEGIN: Metal... Hand...

LENSKY: Can we stop? Is it too late?

ONEGIN: Measure... Pace...

LENSKY: A sane man would run away.

ONEGIN: Will... Steel...

LENSKY: Only an imbecile would stay.

ONEGIN: Nerves... Wire...

LENSKY: Raise, aim, or drop the gun?

ONEGIN: Stop... Aim...

LENSKY: Fire, or turn and run?

ONEGIN: Fire!

LENSKY: No shot disturbs the morning air.
　　No flocks of birds arise,
　　Suddenly as if from nowhere
　　With strident cries.

　　No skull is split between the eyes
　　And no fragmented brain
　　Over the dewy meadow lies
　　To dye the rain.

　　Instead a warm relief is flooding
　　Where the chest is torn apart,

And a well of love is bleeding
From an open heart.

# ELEVEN

*The Empty House.*

TATYANA: Is this the house?
 Heavy drizzle. Leaking walls.
 I pulled the bell.
 Is anyone at home?
 It jangled in the empty hall.
 I hammered the door.
 Is anybody there?
 Shuttered windows, boarded up.
 I made my way to the back.
 Nettles, ivy, bolted grass.
 I forced a window.
 Broke the catch. The curtain tore.
 I dropped inside.
 Smell of damp. Rows of books.
 Leather chair. Burnt lamps.
 I pictured you here,
 Day after day, pacing the room.
 A letter was lying
 Screwed up in the fire-place.
 I went into the hall.
 Stone flags, black and white.
 A yawning bear groped out from the corner
 Half-bald and stuffed.

 I could have come here long ago
 And known you as you really were!

 I went into the billiard-room.
 A cue was out.
 I set a red ball and two white ones.
 We could have played!
 We could have lived!
 I kissed the red.

The door clicked and creaked open. –
This is where he used to spend most of his time.
It was the housekeeper, bent and blind,
A guttering candle welded to her fist. –
I've waited up for him.
His supper's cold.
But he's a wilful one.
He won't be told.

I followed her to the hall.
She wound the clock and set it right.
Bats were darting wall to wall.
I left the house.
The rain had stopped.
The moon was out.
The road ahead
Was flat and grey,
Direct and dead
Mile after mile.

# TWELVE

*Exile.*

ONEGIN: I woke.
   The sun was breaking through the trees.
   The air was still.
   The mist was rising.
   Water was babbling by the mill.
   A horse was grazing by the gate.
   The shrieking birds had flown.

TATYANA: Tuesday I spent in bed
   With a heavy cold in the head.
   Wednesday was taken up with packing,
   Stripping the house and stacking
   Boxes, trunks and cases,
   Some to be taken, some to stay,
   And some to be thrown away.

ONEGIN: I left the mill.
   I left the stream.
   I left the half-
   Remembered dream.
   I left the words.
   I left the lies.
   I'd cut the knot.
   I had no ties.

TATYANA: We sat in silence among the luggage,
   Waiting for the coach. I'd packed my
   Thoughts in crates. The fictions,
   Fantasies and lies were parcelled up
   And lashed. The jagged nerves
   Nails bitten to the quick
   The wasted months, the ball,
   The funeral, and Olga laughing,
   And her wedding,
   And the night Nurse died.

ONEGIN: I swung from one town to another,
　　High as a hawk, as light as air,
　　Scanning the ground and skimming over
　　Lines and layers of daily care,
　　Watching, listening, moving on,
　　Never in any place for long.

TATYANA: The journey was long and bumpy.
　　I wanted to feel sick, but the world
　　Was clattering forward, couldn't
　　Be stopped, and although I was
　　Thrown from side to side,
　　It wasn't an uncomfortable ride.

ONEGIN: Far below me, little lights,
　　Winked and glimmered, waiting there,
　　Flashing signals of despair.
　　Lovers' brawls, domestic fights,
　　The hidden truth, the naked lie,
　　I saw them all and passed them by.

TATYANA: We arrived at night.
　　The lights were bold and bright.
　　Tides of traffic ebbed and swelled,
　　Blanketed in fog that smelled
　　Of perfume and soot.
　　We reached Aunt Alina's
　　By eleven oclock. – How sick you look!
　　You must be hungry! Let me take
　　Your cape. Slip your galoshes off.
　　She rushed around, as thin as a rake
　　With swollen eyes and a hacking cough.

ONEGIN: Men and women by the million,
　　Dragging their weary feet around,
　　In waltz, mazurka and cotillion,
　　Same routine in every town.

TATYANA: The calendar filled with social dates,

Tea parties, soirees, receptions, fetes,
Awash with rakish beaux and bores
And eligible bachelors.

ONEGIN: Vanity dancing with Despair,
Winching in its ageing fat,
Mouthing superficial chat,
Eyes agape in glassy stare.

TATYANA: A gentle general of middling years,
Of ample girth and suitable estate,
Presented me his body, soul and purse
Quietly and politely on a plate.

I pondered his proposal for a day,
And Aunt Alina said she had no doubts,
Exhorting me between her coughing bouts,
To finalize the deal without delay.

I visited the general's family,
Accompanied by a hacking chaperone,
Inspected his propects and pedigree.
Within a month the marriage had begun.

He led me like a sack to his bedroom,
Put out the light and laid me in my front,
Untrussed himself with military aplomb
And did his manly duty with a grunt.

ONEGIN: So I waded place to place,
Watching, listening, staying longer,
Adjudicating the human race,
Indifference giving way to anger,
Lugging my independence round
The social circuit, town to town.
Am I unique? A spirit free?
Or just a rootless refugee,
Slipping down the social world
From one false foothold to another
Back to where we started…?

# THIRTEEN

*Three Years Later.*

TATYANA: Her hair was prematurely flecked with grey.
 Her beauty flourished with the years. She was
 Accounted a success in every way:
 Wife, mother, estate manager, hostess.
 The world delighted in her grand soirees
 And bowed to her authority and charm.

ONEGIN: Who's that? Who is she? Don't I know
 Her face and voice from long ago…?

TATYANA: Her radiant and penetrating gaze
 Could swiftly and effectively disarm,
 Disband, bedazzle and lead by the nose
 A regiment of overbearing beaux!

ONEGIN: The knot of guests in which I mingled
 Asked: To whom did I refer? –
 The lady there. I blushed and tingled,
 Felt my knees belong elsewhere.
 The general beside me roared:
 You're new in town sir, I declare!
 I told him I had been abroad. –
 Then I'll tell you sir, 'pon my life,
 That is no lady, that's my wife!

 Your wife!

TATYANA: How do you do?

ONEGIN: I couldn't speak.

TATYANA: Have you been long in town?

ONEGIN: Two or three days.

TATYANA: We've missed you. Do you plan to stay?

ONEGIN: Her cheek
 Was lightly flushed. She hardly dared to raise

An eyebrow of surprise. – I've travelled wide.

TATYANA: She smiled.

ONEGIN: And I was instantly tongue-tied.
    Was this the blushing bundle of nerve-ends
    That formerly had thrown herself at me?
    How is it that she now so calmly sends
    Me searching for the girl she used to be?

TATYANA: Society demanded her attention,
    At concert, theatre, opera, ballet.
    Her sense of wit and fashionable invention
    Were permanently on public display.

ONEGIN: I read about her in the columns
    Followed her everywhere she went,
    Wrote her letters, reams and volumes,
    Which were signed, sealed up and sent
    With every post. Would she reply,
    Or push them irritably by?

TATYANA: Her carriages propelled her place to place
    And she remained serene despite the pace,
    Amusing the beau monde with her bons mots
    And timing her attendance comme il faut,
    She'd crest the social wave and off she'd go
    To her next tea party or ball or show.

ONEGIN: I know it's not my place to write to you, but I can't
    eat, sleep, think, breathe or exist till I have you back…

TATYANA: She read his stream of letters, didn't reply.
    Her former love was washed up high and dry.

ONEGIN: I know these letters make you angry and you hate
    the way I dog your footsteps and hang on your words. Do
    I want to do this? Do I relish the ribald laughter of your
    friends…?

TATYANA: She salvaged every method she could find
    To put him permanently from her mind.

ONEGIN: Think back! There once was a girl who did the
      same to me, and I was proud, remote. I shrugged you off. I
      fought the truth. I shot my friend...

TATYANA: She bound herself to a rigid routine.
      The house had never been so bright and clean.

ONEGIN: Our love is fated! It has to be! I dread your cold
      stare and your angry sigh, but I have to see you, throw
      myself at your feet! I'm twenty-six! We only have one life!
      It's racing by!

TATYANA: A week went by and then another.
      Then a third, and then a month.
      The letters three or four a day
      Were read, screwed up and thrown away.

ONEGIN: I found myself awake at four o'clock.
      I leapt out of bed and down the stairs,
      Tearing on a coat and out of the door
      And down the frozen street.

TATYANA: Her hair is pulled in vicious pins and grips.
      Her face is heavy with the weight of paint,
      As wearily and slowly she unclips,
      Her body from its bodice's constraint.

ONEGIN: Round a corner, slipped and tripped,
      And skidded, nearly fell,
      Breath steaming in the frost,
      Feet burning with cold.

TATYANA: The fire glows as she applies the cream
      To brow and lid and cheek and lip and chin,
      And wiping off the mask, she dares to dream
      Of shaven face against her milky skin.

ONEGIN: I stopped before the house and looked up.
      A light was shining.

TATYANA: She feels her neck and shoulders bare,
      Unpins and shakes her tumbling hair
      And spying his letter lying there,

She breathes a melancholy prayer.

ONEGIN: The door bursts open!

TATYANA: She turns!

ONEGIN: I had to see you!

TATYANA: She stares!

ONEGIN: I couldn't speak!

TATYANA: I've read your letters, every one.
　　What you want, cannot be done.
　　The girl who loved you has grown up,
　　And though you wanted her to wait,
　　The world went on. It couldn't stop,
　　And now it's too late.

　　She wanted him to rouse her like before,
　　But he was kneeling huddled on the floor.

　　You told me long ago that I
　　Was nothing to you and the lie
　　Has stuck and festered like a dart
　　Embedded in my heart.
　　I've learnt to live with it. I can't
　　Pretend to sentiments that aren't
　　Permitted any more.
　　But I can see that you're
　　Attracted by some new aspect
　　About me, and you can't deflect
　　Your unbecoming wish to be
　　Inferior to me.

　　She wanted him to stand and answer back
　　And so she raised her level of attack.

　　What is it that has made you now
　　Pursue me? Could it be somehow
　　That my estate and social place
　　Are ripe for scandal and disgrace?
　　Do you crave the cheap renown

Of publicly dragging me down?
Where is dignity? At least
Before, your coldness carried weight.
But now you cower like a beast.
Your letters are so desolate!

She felt a sudden well of pity rise
Filling behind the flood-gates of her eyes.

If you could only see me as
I used to be. But that is past.
You only want me now that I
Am elevated. That it why
I cannot love you I'm afraid.
This gaudy dance and cheap parade
Mean nothing to me. I'd be glad
To lose them all and live in peace…

It's morning now.
You're free to go.
I loved you once.
I love you still.
But I am now
Another's wife,
And I am bound to him
For life.

ONEGIN: She rose and left the room. He remained still,
Then slowly rose and walked to the window.
The leaves were budding in the morning chill
And birds were leaving foot-prints in the snow.
He saw her leave the house and walk along
The terrace, down the steps, across the lawn.
His heart was light. His head was clear and free.
A swing was hanging from an ancient tree,
Suspended there for children long ago.
He stood there for a long time behind the glass
Watching her swinging gently to and fro.

*The End.*

# GOGOL

Richard Crane as Gogol, Royal Court (photo: Andrew Ward)

*Gogol* was first performed for the Brighton Actors' Workshop at the Marlborough Hotel, Brighton, 16th April 1978, directed and designed by Faynia Williams, performed by the author.

It was premiered in London in September 1979, by the English Stage Company at the Royal Court Theatre, directed and designed by Faynia Williams, performed by the author.

Produced by Brighton Theatre, Faynia Williams' production toured the UK, Poland, Sweden, Russia, Australia and the USA, including the Edinburgh, Adelaide, Belfast, Brighton, Stratford, Glasgow and other Festivals. Brighton Theatre's *Gogol* represented Britain at the Britain Salutes New York Festival, 1983.

As *Le Jour de la Limace*, it was presented at L'Espace Acteur, Paris in January 1988, on Radio France Culture and Sveriges Riksradio. It was performed by Freddie Jones, directed by Alfred Bradley on BBC Radio 3, March 1979.

# PART ONE

*A man seated on a stool, clean and neat, in a threadbare brown coat which is held together by paper-clips.*

I'm neither tall nor short. I'm not fat; I'm not thin. I'm neither old nor young. I'm not fair; I'm not dark. I'm neither fighting fit, nor prone to sickness; not well off, not hard up; not good-looking, not bad looking either; not clever, not dim; not too happy, not too sad; not generous, not mean; not precise, not vague; not extreme either one way or the other.

I think that's a fair description without giving too much away.

In other words, I'm middle height, average weight, middle income, average intelligence, middle class, average age, and on the whole, fairly content. Thirty-five seconds.

I'm well aware I'm lacking in certain areas. I don't have a wife and family, or a car, or domestic pets. I'm not a home owner. I have no parents. I don't take holidays abroad. I don't have a Visa card, central heating or a garden.

People I know who have these things, are forever hinting to me that my life is not complete – or rather hinting to each other. Being self-contained, I'm seldom in a position to be addressed directly. I don't avoid talking to others. Conversely, I don't make a point of it, except to correct the odd misconception, for instance, that I'm a social outcast, in need of sympathy. Why do they do it? They're not concerned about me. They're only concerned to *appear* concerned. I've even heard them expressing concern about each other's concern. If I really needed them, they'd be so concerned, they'd be unavailable. One minute twenty seconds.

Monday to Friday I get up at ten to seven. I wash, do my teeth, wet shave, go to the toilet; dress, brush my hair – all the time listening to news and views on the radio, and avoiding over-close contact with my image in the mirror. Why do I do that? What's the temptation? I once gave into it and was mesmerized for half an hour, consequently missing my bus and chasing minutes all day. The fact is, in all respects, I am average, middle-grade, well-contained and regular, with one exception, which ignore it as I might, is always with me. I don't want to dwell on it. Over the years, it has developed a self-importance which has no need of encouragement. It's there, every time I look down, demanding attention. It's long, fleshy, arrogant, rubbery, cavernous, cacophonous, and prone to spots and blackheads. It sniffs and snorts, pokes itself into other people's affairs. It runs. It tickles. It sneezes in public. It's a constant menace. Keep going, don't stop. I make porridge, I make tea, I pour some fruit juice and make toast. I bring in the milk and the paper. I'm sitting down to breakfast by twenty to eight. Two and a half minutes.

Half way. I haven't begun to review last week, let alone plan for next. This happens every time. I get side-tracked. I've been doing this every Sunday for seven years. At five to twelve, I sit down in my coat and talk to myself non-stop for five minutes, prior to starting the new week with a brisk turn around the park. It began as therapy for a speech impediment. It's also a useful method of examining where I've been and what I've done since we last met, and what I intend doing about it.

Thirdly, it helps me to come to terms with Sunday: the Day of the Slug; the day with no spine. Ever since God retired, there's been no reason for it. Ninety percent have no use for it. If only people would realize this instead of pretending! One seventh of life is wasted. Assuming a life-span of seventy, that's ten years! It's more than a waste: it's a vacuum. It sucks you down, if you don't keep a tight grip on yourself. The vast majority of suicides occur on Sundays. I don't know if that's a fact. I don't have access to the figures, but it's a theory I'll hold to, until it's proved otherwise.

I got my job on the understanding that if I stuck to it,
Monday to Friday, nine to five, with an hour for lunch,
twelve-thirty to one-thirty, I'd be safely installed for forty-
two years, with no variation in pace of work and income
level-pegged with inflation to the best of the Board's ability.
Upon this rock, my life is built. Rains may descend and
floods come and beat upon my life, and I shall continue,
waking, walking, working, feeding and sleeping, for as
long as nothing disturbs my timetable. The week-days, by
and large, take care of themselves. Occasionally, there's
forty minutes to an hour to be filled, and I can meet this
well enough with a crossword or a game of patience.
On Saturdays, I can, as a rule, stretch the cleaning,
shopping and laundry, to cover four hundred and twenty
working minutes, while reserving the hours of evening
for household accounts. Then just as I'm settling back, in
control of myself, and pleased that I've completed a full
week without diversions or uncertainties – Sunday comes!
It's always waiting: like a pit! I don't have a car to wash,
or a dog to walk, or a lawn to mow, or children to take to
relatives. I have to invent activities to keep my mind and
body from corroding, and more often than not, I find an
average imagination, is not sufficient to meet this challenge.

It's so cold these days. I have to go out in all weathers.
I ought to walk further on Sundays, but there's not the
incentive. I could take advantage of amenities laid on, and
visit the Tower of London, or go to the pictures, but the
position is, I'm not equipped for the risks. I stick to the
path, I don't look round, I cannot stop to help, I cannot be
approached *even* for directions to such-and-such a street.
My knowledge of local geography is strictly limited. I have
no wish to increase it. I know just enough to get me from
my room to my work, from my work to my room, and
briskly around the park on a Sunday. I'm not a policeman.
I'm not a social worker, and I'm not obliged to give
charity, because I don't have a conscience. I'm illegitimate.
I wasn't required. I was to have been aborted, but there

were rules in those days, when God was still in office, and my mother wasn't equipped to break them.

I'm not going to waste time wondering what my father was like. It's only on Sundays that the possibility of him even occurs to me. He was probably as average and self-contained as I am. If I put my mind to it, I would come to the conclusion that in his position, I would have done exactly the same. There's only one thing that horrifies me and that's the thought of dependants. I take after my father, inasmuch as neither of us really care where we come from or whom we take after. My mother used to say I had his nose. I grew up under the impression that the thing I sniffed with was somehow on a long-term loan, and one day I would be called upon to give it back. I used to believe that the reason my father never showed his face was because he was so ashamed not to have a nose on it.

On Wednesday, I got up late. I normally wake at twelve minutes to seven: two minutes before my alarm. For some reason it hadn't gone off. It was half past! I've had a number of clocks. I've always found that in time, they fail me. I need a clock to monitor my routine and all I ask is that it functions according to its trade description. My problem – and I see no immediate way of solving it – is that within my fixed income bracket, I am not able to purchase a mechanism competitive with my own physical workings. If I was prone to flattery, I'd be pleased at this: to know that no man-made chronometer can keep up with me. On the other hand, it could just be a reflection on the declining standard of workmanship.

I shot out of bed and knocked it over. The alarm rang. I picked it up, folded it – it was still ringing – and snapped it shut. It's a travel clock, purchased from a chemist on my birthday, by the one person who doggedly remembers year after year. It was easy to buy, the chemist being on my route. I didn't need to digress. I allowed ten minutes and did it in seven – three minutes gained! And the bus was early. I normally count on five minutes waiting, during which time I stare downwards and shut my ears to the comments: Where does he live? How old is he? What's his background? It came in *four*! I'd saved a minute! It slipped along the bus lane. It drove like a dream. I was up in the office with seven minutes to spare!

That's what it is to be ahead of time: to get there first; to go to the window and look down; to find, on your birthday, you've *gained* a year and not lost it! The Final Demands room is on the seventeenth floor. Seven minutes for looking down. To see it all going on fifty yards below, the living network in full rhythm: sliding, weaving, surging, filtering, intersecting, powered and driven by one force! To watch it in miniature beyond the glass, and to know that for seven minutes, you're not part of it! What makes it go? Who winds it up? How long will it last? Who is it for?

I take home ninety-nine pounds a week, which I divide neatly into three parts: thirty-three pounds for rent and rates, thirty-three for living expenses, and thirty-three for bills and other contingencies. I keep an itemized account of income and expenditure with notes in the margin on price rises, discounts and bargain offers.

Even now I can hear them whispering: Why is he quiet? Why is he so contained? Why is he never absent? Why is he so tidy? Why is he never negligent? Why is he so precise?

There was a girl at the bus-stop on Thursday. She couldn't have been more than sixteen.

Who does he mix with? What has he done? He's hiding his past. It's a terrible thing loneliness. He'll regret it when he's old. He'll be sorry when he's ill. What are his feelings when he wakes up at three o'clock in the morning, sweating and shivering? He's only himself to blame. No man is an island.

I have a Friend who never speaks. He comforts me. He covers me against the cold. He comes with me to work. He comes home with me every night. He wraps himself around me. He knows my needs, my habits, my temperature, all my physical details. When he tears, I mend him. If he frays, I patch him. When he is soiled, I have him cleaned. He never shows me up.

I'm not watching the clock. It's let me down once this week. I'm relying on instinct. The long-term purpose of these soliloquies is to train myself to continue walking the tight-rope when the safety-net has been whipped away, as it is every Sunday: not to look down, not to stop, not to wonder: why is nothing happening, what is the purpose, what will I do after forty-two years continuous employment, when every day will be a Sunday, every week will be a year, and every thought, word and deed will be directed towards ways and means of filling the silence.

Sometimes I think I've mastered it. One Sunday, about a year ago, I was so full of things to say, I went on for two and a half hours! The words came running and jumping and tumbling over each other, in wisecracks, aphorisms, figures of speech, whole subjects in nutshells, making logical patterns in simple syntax and all of it together making perfect sense. The room was thick with wisdom. The walls were dripping with wit. The air was intoxicating and stung the eyes, and lifted me right out of my body, so I could look and see what I was: a composite unit of feet, legs, arms, hands, belly, chest, face. The eyes were streaming. The mouth was working nineteen to the dozen: clicking, popping, spouting, gurgling, like a knitting machine exuding miles of multi-coloured fabric. And in-between, there was nothing: a flat space between the cheeks.

The door-bell rang. I never expect callers. I shot back to my place above the upper lip, and the magic stopped. The walls were dry. The air was sober, and the words disappeared like bubbles. It was a woman from my work. I don't know her name. She has a black wart on her neck and loose muscles under her eyes. She was just passing, might she drop in, did I mind, awful weather, she lived alone, I did too, did I have parents, nor did she, spinster, bachelor, rising prices, cost of living, bus fares! How did I cope? She knew the cause: the unions, what could one do, vandalism, can't go out, capital punishment, television, moral fibre, switch it off, what did I think, exactly, is that the time, did I ever, see me tomorrow, bye!

Her face was round like a newlaid egg. She was at the bus-stop on Thursday; same again on Friday. She had a plastic carrier-bag full of shopping: sliced bread, tea-bags, frozen peas, vermicelli and half a dozen eggs. How old is she? I wouldn't put her above sixteen.

It's the worst winter on record. I put my coat on the other day and split the lining. I mended it, put it on, and split the sleeve. My coat is disintegrating in direct proportion to the increasing harshness of the weather. I mended it, put it on, and the back split. Having run out of cotton, I held it together with paper-clips. I had three minutes to recoup as I hurried to the bus, moving only my feet. I called at the haberdasher's for some cotton. It's on my route; I didn't need to digress. I explained the situation. The woman roared with laughter. Clouds of steam escaped her mouth in the freezing shop. I had to tell her it was not her position to advise a customer as to what he should wear. My shoulder split as I made my purchase. I'd lost a minute and a couple of paper-clips. They wouldn't allow me on the bus. They said it was full. I could see space for at least three persons of average bulk, which was occupied, as I was speaking, by a pregnant woman who elbowed past me with her child.

I've never allowed weather conditions to prevent me getting to work. I've always regarded getting to work as necessary as eating and breathing.

The food in her bag was an indication of the life she led. The look on her face took my breath away. She was brittle as an egg.

No one said anything about my coat. I hung it up in the cloakroom. I tried to apologize for being late, but half the staff weren't there, including the Department Supervisor. I registered and dispatched twenty-seven Final Demands, and twelve Official Notices to Occupiers, indicating the cutting off of power supply, in consequence of non-payment of account.

Next week will be like any other. I don't foresee any changes. Last week was like the one before: no amendments made, no corners turned. The only outstanding business is my alarm-clock, to be collected and paid for on Thursday. There's also my coat...

It's ten past twelve! I've overshot by ten minutes! I wouldn't count myself a paragon of exactitude. At the same time, I am required by my work, not to countenance wastage. There have been times when I have left a light on, even the bar of a fire on one occasion, but I've always made a point of making it up. Last winter I sat for a whole Sunday, in my coat, with no heating, to make up for units wasted in neglecting to switch off my towel-rail.

All this means I shall have to curtail my walk by half, which as it happens is just as well, because I don't know if my coat could take it.

# PART TWO

*Standing on the stool in a large, important, fur-collared coat.*

I'm tall, stout, healthy, successful, well-off, good-looking, intelligent and fascinating. I grow an inch every twenty-four hours. Today I'm six foot three. I've been late for work every day this week. On Wednesday I was forty minutes late. No one dares to question me because I'm so tall.

You'll notice I'm speaking directly to an audience. I'm pitching my voice so that everyone can hear. Every Sunday, at five to twelve, I gather together my critics, disciples, enemies and friends, and harangue them non-stop for five minutes, prior to striding through the park, striking terror into children, dogs, prams, footballs.

Remember that girl at the bus-stop? She's still there. She's so thin, she's beginning to look like a bus-stop.

The thing about working in my particular field is that you mustn't become involved with the consumer. You're not dealing with people, not even with money. It's figures. If they don't match, you switch off. Any concern for the human element is extraneous to the job guide-lines, and the social services, whose function it is, to mop up hypothermia and malnutrition, won't thank you for it. Our job is to administer commas, colons and full-stops upon the consumer's copy-book from a non-emotive stand-point fifty yards up. Some less tenacious colleagues of mine, have wilted in the face of pleas from old folk and mothers with young children. They have to pay or be cut off! If you fudge the logic of that, you're betraying the formula upon which our collective life is founded, and which decrees that if you weaken, you have to be rooted out to join the very same sad heap you were foolish enough to express pity for. We had an instance of this the other day. A clerk in the Final Demands Department, out of pity, had been secretly slipping decimal points in sums payable, one digit to the left, thus reducing remittances by ninety percent and rupturing the system. It so happened that an honest consumer complained about this, and the fraud was unearthed. The woman lost control, hurled obscenities at the Department Supervisor, and had her employment terminated.

There is someone in the Department, being paid to monitor efficiency. There's going to be a pruning of staff. A certain percentage will have to go. This person is being paid to keep his eyes open and recommend names for dismissal. Since the rumour developed, everyone's been creeping about like mice. They think it's me. They're falling over each other to be nice to me. But I keep my distance; you have to, with a coat like mine. I bought it last week with my savings. Over the years I've made a practice of putting by a few pence each week. At the beginning of last week, I had seventy-nine pounds.

People tend to give way to me when they see my coat – with one exception. We collided as we stepped onto the bus and her eggs fell out. I asked her where her manners were, and that was the start of our conversation.

We were crushed together in the bus, just a bursting carrier-bag between us. She was so brittle, I thought she'd break. She was screaming at me for suggesting she had no manners. The bus was jam-packed and dead silent, as she tore into me for breaking her eggs. Fury spat in my face: a hailstorm of stinging darts at point-blank range. For weeks I'd watched her at the bus-stop, and developed the opinion she was a doll, made of eggshell and chicken-bones. Now all my compressed attention was exploding back at me. In all my life, no one had ever even established my existence. She was giving me all I had lacked since the day I was born: this brittle thing, this newlaid egg. It went on for hours, days, weeks, like an aria, with the *sotto voce* chorus of the jam-packed bus; until finally we arrived at my destination and slithered off.

I didn't look back. I walked along my route. I never look back. I wasn't going to change my habit. I was thrilled, scalding hot, my feet churning the slush, and my coat retaining my body-heat like tank-lagging. I could feel her coming up behind me. She was walking along beside me. I knew that wasn't her stop – she always travelled further. Slow down! She was laughing! Slow down, slow *down*! We stopped.

Would you tell when I've completed five minutes? I tend not to watch the clock nowadays, being as I am, in the business of demonstrating that time is a servant, not a master. I can't promise I'll stop directly. I may be in full flight on a vital topic. I may be half-way down a blind alley, but I'll endeavour to take note and draw, with dignity, to a close.

I'm bored with the Department: not the work, the people. They hold things up. They have no commitment to their work. They treat it like a club. They waste their time and the Board's money, just as the consumers we deal with are wasting energy. Over the past week it has slowly dawned on me that every one of my colleagues is superfluous. I know their duties. I know how every area of the Department functions, and this is my plan! Cut the lunch-break by half, add an hour in the morning and an hour in the evening, take home two hours' worth of filing to be completed before going to bed, and six hours' to be completed at the week-end, and I can do it all! It would be a saving in wages to the Board of one thousand three hundred and eighty pounds a week, which is five thousand five hundred and twenty pounds a month, which is sixty-six thousand two hundred and forty pounds a year; and if this procedure were to be adopted through all the departments of which there are twenty-four, the total annual saving to the Board, in this region alone, would be to the tune of one million five hundred and ninety-eight thousand seven hundred and sixty pounds, which could then be ploughed back in reduction of tariff to the consumer, thus further decreasing the workload and instituting exponential economies in all departments, insofar as the need to follow up Second, Further and Final Demands, would be less pressing. It would also ease the burden on the social services, inasmuch as fewer consumers would be placed in conditions of distress, and so ultimately, be of benefit to the taxpayer.

I saw this coat in a window one day, when my old coat was falling off my back. It was away from my route. I had to digress; and in those days, digression was a horrifying prospect. My pattern of life was so strict, any departure from it was like an expedition to the South Pole.

I slipped out in my lunch-break. The snow plastered me as I trudged. The streets were a whirling white blanket. The traffic was at a stand-still. I'd mapped out my route to the shop which I had seen advertised in a newspaper. I was the only moving thing. It was mid-day in the heart of town. I was the only creature, human, animal or mechanical, that dared to penetrate that blizzard. I had half an hour and seventy-nine pounds in my pocket. I got to the shop. In the window was the coat. It stared at me. It glowed in the cold. I'd seen it before: only once, from the rear. I'd never seen it from the front. It was when I was a child. I was up in my room. I'd heard shouting and weeping and crashing glass. A man was downstairs. My mother was screaming. The front door slammed. I ran to the window and saw the coat, walking away down the street.

You've got his nose: nothing else, just his nose. Before she died, she gave me nine hundred and ninety-nine pounds. She was quite serious; it wasn't a joke. She said: Put it towards the expense of changing your nose.

One by one, we put the lights out. As far as the Department is concerned, that's it, that's the end. The consumer no longer consumes. He is cut off, dead. I keep a map on my wall and stick black-headed pins in addresses we have cut off. As a rule, these tend to cluster in densely populated areas. It's not difficult to see a new process at work for the levelling of numbers, which is more humane than natural selection by epidemics and disasters. It's also easier to operate: just a flick of the switch. What annoys me about my colleagues is lack of vocation. They will not accept that our work is sacred. They'll regret it. The day before yesterday, I sent a Final Demand to the woman who was sacked.

We stood there laughing, not a stone's throw from the bus-stop. I'm having a party, said the Egg, next Saturday. Why not come along? She wrote her address on the back of my hand, because neither of us had any paper.

It's you, isn't it, said a nervous colleague, as I fastened another paper-clip onto my old coat, prior to leaving. – What's me? – You know, the rumour that's been going around. – I don't listen to rumours. – Nor do I, but one can't help it can one, when one's job is at stake? She went on: I've been with the Department twenty-three years. I'm due for retirement when I'm sixty. If I lost my job now, I don't know what I'd do. I've never fiddled my bills like some I could mention – except just the once, a couple of months ago, but I've made it up, you'll tell them I've made it up, every penny, I promise you. Don't you need a new coat?

The coat in the window was ninety-nine pounds. I was twenty pounds short. Next day on my desk, I found an envelope. I opened it in the toilet. It contained two ten-pound notes. For the rest of the day I was conscious of the clatter of nervous winking from the woman in the far corner. A few days later, when I appeared in the coat, the clatter of her right eyelid had achieved such a level of blinking sonority, I was obliged to cast her a swift reproving glance.

I have made an appointment to see the Supervisor after lunch on Friday. He said he wanted a word with me anyway. It's too late to get my nose done for the party on Saturday. The operation takes several days, from beginning to end, and there's bound to be a waiting list. I'm very much afraid that when I kiss her, the sheer bulk of my nose will break her shell. We may have to dispense with kissing. I want to wrap myself and her chicken-bones in my coat. I want to roll and roll downhill until we're six feet thick in a ball of snow and no one can see what we're doing.

Tomorrow is Monday of the week I come alive. The next day is Tuesday. I shall be six foot five. The dustman comes on Wednesday. Buried in tea-leaves and potato peelings is the corpse of my Friend. It was a mercy killing. He was beyond repair. I simply removed the paper-clips and he was thankful to be at peace.

On Thursday I shall count every second and cross it off on my clock. On Friday is my interview with the Supervisor. I shall tell him, in confidence, of my plan for streamlining the Department. He must know I've been thinking of it, which is why he wants to see me.

On Saturday I shall make my way to the address on my hand. I know what to do. I've devoted a lifetime of abstinence to the preparation for this encounter, so there is no contingency I am not fully equipped for. You can rest assured I have everything planned, right through to fertilizing her egg.

How long have I had? I'm sorry, I did ask if someone would tell me when I'd completed five minutes. I find increasingly there aren't enough hours in the day and minutes in the hour and seconds in the minute to accommodate what I have to do, and if no one has the courage to pull me up short, I race ahead. I can't stopped.

When I left school, I had nine hundred and ninety-nine pounds inherited from my mother. I bought a car. I learnt to drive. My aim was to cross the Channel and speed my way right around the world, prior to deciding what to do with my life. I'd wait for no one. I'd make no plans. I'd drive with the roof off, and the wind in my hair, as countries and continents flicked by, the world spinning under me like a top, my heart pounding with excitement because at last, I was responsible to no one, and no one and nothing depended on me! I sang! I filled the air!

*(Sings.)* Old Abram Brown is dead and gone,
you'll never see him more!
He used to wear a long brown coat
that buttoned down before – !

I'm going too fast. It's too late to stop. I can't be checked. You missed your chance. I gave you warning. You didn't speak up. You sat like dummies. I talked and talked. I'm coming towards you. I'm speeding like light across miles and miles of driven snow, hurled onward by a whistling wind across a frozen sea! I'm breaking the minutes, bursting the hours, crashing the weeks! I'm coming to the mainland, so fast you can't see me: a great Nose in a Coat, like a spiralling typhoon! I can't be stopped! Faster, faster! Get back! Mind out! *MIIIIIIIIIIIIND AAAAAAAAAAAAOOOUT!!!*

# PART THREE

*Crouched in grey underwear, hugging his knees, inside the upturned stool.*

The car was written off. I was unconscious for several days. I've heard it said that I suffered brain damage and as a result am unfit for positions of responsibility. This is nonsense. When I awoke from the accident, I had a vision of life so comprehensive, I couldn't even speak about it. They took my silence as proof that I was defective. I have now found my voice.

I have to keep talking, I can't stop, but the words are metered. I can't pay for them. Eighty-six.

Cheques and postal orders should be made payable to the Board and crossed "payment by cheque". Please detach the counterfoil at the foot of the account and send it with your cheque, keeping the detailed account for your records. No receipt will be given unless you specifically request it, by ticking the box overleaf *and* sending the complete account. One three seven.

This is the position I favour for conserving energy. It brings me face to face with my knees. Even though it obliges me to be two foot tall, at the same time it is vitally important, when the going is rough, to be in constant correspondence with one's outlying regions by the shortest possible route. Take for instance the passing of a message from the brain to the feet. In the old days, it could take a week, having to progress in stages through the neck to the chest and the belly hips and legs, which when account is taken of diversions down the arm to the hand, and unscheduled lingerings in the stomach, amounts to a very major and perilous expedition indeed. The new improved method, of which I am the progenitor and exponent, entirely bypasses the abdominal connection, and allows a clear unhindered passage. Of course you may retort that the time saved by this improvement scheme may well be countered by the impediment to motion necessarily imposed upon a body in such a restrictive posture, and I must admit I haven't as yet come up with an answer to that one, but I'm working on it.

I expect everyone is longing to know how my interview went with the Supervisor. And I imagine there's a fair deal of predatory interest as to how the party went on Saturday.

Members of our staff are at your service to give advice or assistance. If you are not satisfied with the way a personal enquiry has been dealt with, please write to your District Manager. Four two three.

Sometimes I have to listen to what they're saying: the lice that eat up my floorboards. They talk so loudly, there's no avoiding it. In the absence of factual information, which I will never give to anyone, except on the confidential record-of-personnel form, which is completed at the end of lunch-break for immediate filing; in the absence of the facts, they compose a fantasia of falsehoods and fiddle-di-dees, trilled out to the accompaniment of fingernails on emery boards.

I have a head, a body, two arms, two legs, two pairs of shoes which I heel and sole twice yearly, a brain; I *did* have a coat, a nose on a long-term loan...

I don't know where it's gone. I woke up on Friday, looked in the mirror – it wasn't there! It was the day of my interview with the Supervisor. It's an unwritten rule in the Department that everyone presents himself with a full set of regulation features, and I have always been the first person to uphold this. When the woman who was sacked for decimal point transference arrived one morning without her teeth, and an inarticulate account of how her allergy to the house-dust-mite had caused her to sneeze them down her newly-installed and fully-operative waste-disposal unit, I was the first to shoot her a glance of the severest reproval. With proper care, this need never have happened, and I was the first to connect her flippant attitude to the affair, with a basic unsuitability for work in our Department.

I searched for an hour. I ransacked my room, searched in all pockets, went through the dustbin with a tooth-comb. One thing I did find was my scarf. I muffled my face and went out to meet the Supervisor.

Come in! The Black Wart With The Loose Eye Muscles was sitting beside him. It took me four seconds to put two and two together. It was *her*: the spy that was being paid to collect names!

According to Miss Hairy Black Wart With The Bloody Eyeballs – I can never remember names! – I'd been late without leave on twelve occasions in the past fortnight. My output had deteriorated to the point where it was clear I had no continuing interest in the Department.

Ah but, I retorted, I have a plan that will save the Board in this region alone an annual sum of one million five hundred and eighty-nine thousand seven hundred and sixty pounds!

My attitude to my colleagues had been surly and dismissive, creating feelings which were detrimental to the work and could only indicate, to put it bluntly, that I was in the wrong job.

Cut the lunch-break by half, add an hour in the morning and an hour in the evening, and I can do it all!

Now we are instructed to effect a cutback in staff. I'm sure you'll understand, we do not wish to have to do this. At the same time we cannot carry a workforce which is not prepared to pull its weight. We're going to have to terminate your employment.

I can see from this position, that the world is very often the wrong way up. Being round and continually turning, spinning like a top, it's not really surprising that the poles are interchangeable: that the legs are in fact the arms, that the knees are really elbows, and that the north cheeks are easily confused with the south cheeks. If I were a psychogeologist, I'd have a lot to say about the nose and the penis, Great Britain and New Zealand, the gullet and the rectum, Hudson Bay and Lake Victoria.

I received my education from a man I respected, with a squint, who couldn't keep order. He was delicate, in spite of his brute face, with a broken nose from a fight he had with a corporal in the army who said he saw him nosing his little lady-love, who as it turned out, was the regimental harlot. This man, the day before he was sacked, told me in confidence about life, death, work, art, money, other people and God: an education for life in one afternoon! It took my breath away.

You appear to have overlooked payment of your account and it would be helpful if you would give this matter your immediate attention. It is of course possible that you may have paid the account in full during the preparation of this reminder, in which case please accept the Board's apology. One five nine four.

I never saw any reason for this. We weren't paid to apologize. It was a prerequisite of the job to have no feelings of any kind. I would have rephrased this section but I wasn't qualified.

My school was an operating theatre. They laid me on a slab, slit my nose, extracted my imagination in strands and slopped it in the pedal-bin. It's no disgrace. There's no stigma to being unimaginative. It makes economic sense to feel you no longer have to cap the next man's bright ideas. You're fully taken care of. Everything is provided, and should you ever at any time be in any doubt as to how to react or what to consume, kindly consult your television.

This morning, my Nose came back: naked and very small. He slipped himself through the letter-box and landed on the door-mat. I tried to reach, but the muscles had gone.

He'd taken my invitation and borrowed my coat so she would recognize him. As it happens, it was was no skin off *my* nose because (a) I hadn't got one, and (b) I don't think I'd have gone to the party anyway.

The Nose in the Coat strode off across the park. He walked all the way. He'd allowed an hour and did it in forty minutes! He rang the door-bell. No answer… He rang the door-bell. The snow had thawed: heaps of slush on the pavement. No answer… He rang the door-bell. A trio of icicles descended from the guttering and just missed him. No answer… He rang the door – It opened…

She stood there in a towel, much fatter than he ever imagined. Look you're too early. Nothing happen till after the pubs close. You wouldn't like to get yourself a drink and come back later?

Since my interview with the Supervisor, I've been serving a month's notice. But they won't allow me to go to work! They're afraid I might come up with some home truths.

He sat in the pub with half a pint. He drank it very slowly for two and a half hours.

That the whole thing is a pretence, and I was given my cards because I called their bluff. When I awoke from my accident, I was dumb. I can now speak. *The world is winding down!* Certain people know this – the ones that moved God into retirement. Most people, who have had the imaginationectomy, don't know a thing. Now it's most important for the ones that *do* know, to maintain the pretence. Otherwise there might be panic. My scheme for the Department, which I was not allowed to propose, would have held back the winding down and afforded a breathing-space…

He was about to ring the door – It flew open. I appear to be late. I'm a friend of… He was sucked inside, had his coat removed – Mind my coat if you don't mind! – and beer splashed over him and a bread-roll poked in his eye. Everyone was talking; no one was listening. Everyone knew everyone; no one knew him. I'm a friend of the girl… A pair of breasts flattened his nose. A pale young man pushed past into a corner and vomited on the coats. The girl who's responsible, I never remember names... He couldn't see her, didn't know if he'd recognize her, wondered why on earth he'd ever come and if he'd ever get out. Will you tell her I'm sorry – he was being edged inwards towards the stairs – but I've got to go... A boy and a girl were kissing against the banisters. A man muscled through with a brace of pints. I have to get back... The kissing girl swung round and shot her tongue like a torpedo down his throat! Don't push me, I'm squashed... And beer spouted in all directions as the muscling man lost his footing – Let me out! – and the hallway exploded into laughter and shrieks!

Which is why they keep sending notices. They want me dead. If you are not satisfied with the advice and assistance of our staff, and if, having written to your Area Manager, you remain dissatisfied, and if having contacted the Consultative Council, you decline to accept its findings, then you are clearly prevaricating beyond the bounds permitted by the Board and fully deserve what's coming to you.

She was upstairs alone in a small room. Her face was plucked, her hair swept up. Her lips were purple. Her eyes were black. She couldn't have been less than thirty.

Thought I'd frightened you off. You don't know anyone do you? Have you had a drink? It's my birthday. It's so depressing. Where's you face?

There was a man lying on her bed like a white slug.

You know what I am don't you? What made you come here? God I wish I didn't have to live. This place is being pulled down, did you know that? They're going to get an iron weight and swing it against the wall.

I don't know how I found my coat, but I did. I don't how it wasn't soiled with beer and vomit, but somehow it was still intact. I don't know how I got out without being asphyxiated or torn to shreds.

Which way had I come? Was it through the stomach, or directly from the knees to the face? I couldn't remember. It seemed so long ago. And there wasn't this fog…

Which way was the main road? The sea was frozen over when I left the island, which was why my journey was so swift. I never imagined it might thaw. For the first time in my life, I hadn't allowed for the future.

Fog… Visibility three feet. They were all people who hadn't paid their bills. They were no longer connected to the central motor. They were cut off, drifting loose.

Fog… One foot six. What did I see in her? Why was she ruined? Why do eggs go bad? If you prick them either end and blow out the inside, they last for ever. They look just the same. You don't know they're hollow till you touch them.

Fog… Where am I? Where's the road? Where are the houses? Where am I going?

I have a Friend who never speaks. He comforts me. He covers me against the fog…

Who's that? Who's there…? I'm sorry, I can't see you… I sorry I don't stop… Please let me pass… I have to get home –

*I AM SELF-CONTAINED! I NEVER TAKE SIDES! I'M HAPPY AS I AM!*

They jumped on me, knocked me over, I got up, they kicked me, I fell. They picked me up and punched me in the stomach. I doubled up; they pulled me back. They tore at my coat and ripped the buttons. I struggled and kicked. They wrenched the collar and the sleeves, they tugged at the shoulders. I pulled away and fell down. They dragged it from me…

This is the best position I can think of for keeping warm. Since they cut me off, I've been trying to retain what heat I can, though I'm well aware it's a futile exercise, because technically speaking, I no longer exist.

Put your hand on my stomach and you can feel my spine.

I'm holding on to every degree of my temperature, but one by one they're slipping away. I'm clenching my mouth but the words leak out through the hole in my face.

Did you know they can train pigeons to read? Did you know that with a system of rewards and punishments, they can train people to read and write? Pigeons can't write, but it's only a matter of time. Could you let me know when I've completed seventy years? Did you know pigeons can fly? Except when they're too busy reading.

Today is Sunday. So is tomorrow. And the day after.

Did you know they put God away? He'd gone too far. He was beginning to be unpredictable. Unfortunately he is the only one who knows the answer. He is the only one who knows how to stop the winding-down. No one has the courage to bring him back. He may have lost confidence.

Did you know there are four "O"s in my name? They've taken away the consonants.

I shouldn't be talking. Words are finite. But the more I talk, the less I think. And the more I think, the less I am.

*Light begins to fade very slowly.*

There are thirty-eight years to go, which is thirteen thousand eight hundred and seventy days, plus nine point five for leap years, which is three hundred and thirty-three thousand, one hundred and eight hours, which is one thousand, one hundred and ninety-nine million, one hundred and eighty-eight thousand, eight hundred seconds, approximately. Now given an average of three words per second, the very maximum I shall require, assuming I talk as I eat and never sleep, and allowing a twelve percent contingency is four thousand and twenty-nine million, two hundred and seventy-four thousand three hundred and sixty-eight words. Now given that I require nought point one five units of heat to generate each word, and heat is bought at a rate of two point five one pence per unit, the estimated overall energy cost to continue speaking for the rest of my life, hypothetically speaking, because in reality I and the world will be long dead by then, will be one thousand five hundred and sixteen million, seven hundred and seventy thousand, seven hundred and ninety-nine pounds, fifty-five point two pence, not allowing for inflation...

*Blackout.*

*The End.*

# SATAN'S BALL

## FROM BULGAKOV'S
## MASTER AND MARGARITA

Poster design by Dan Sneider

# Characters

The parts are divided between 15 actors as follows:

1.     IVAN NIKOLAYEVICH BEZDOMNY – writer
   MATTHEW- ex-tax-collector
   AUDIENCE MEMBER/BALL GUEST

2.     MIKHAIL ALEXANDROVICH BERLIOZ – Chairman of
   the Writers' Union
   DR. STRAVINSKY – psychiatrist
   PUBLISHER
   GEORGE BENGALSKY – Master of Ceremonies
   AUDIENCE MEMBER

3.     PONTIUS PILATE – Procurator of Judea
   AUDIENCE MEMBER/BALL GUEST

4.     SECRETARY – to Pilate
   PRASKOVYA FYODOROVNA – psychiatric nurse
   AUDIENCE MEMBER/BALL GUEST

5.     YESHUA HA-NOTSRI – vagrant preacher
   THE MASTER

6.     MARK MURIBELLUM – centurion
   POLICE OFFICER/SECURITY GUARD
   AUDIENCE MEMBER

7.     WOLAND – Maestro of Black Magic

8.     HELLA – witch-demon

9.     BEHEMOTH – cat-demon

10.    AZAZELLO – boy-demon

11.    ARCHIBALD ARCHIBALDOVICH – committee member
    CAIAPHAS – High Priest
    BYSTANDER/AUDIENCE MEMBER
    LATUNSKY – critic
    BORIS MIKHAILOVICH – Margarita's husband

12.    NASTASYA LUKINISHNA – committee member
       BYSTANDER/AUDIENCE MEMBER
       STAGE MANAGER/CLERK
       LAPSHENNIKOVA – critic

13.    TAMARA POLUMESYATZ – committee member
       BYSTANDER/AUDIENCE MEMBER
       DEPUTY STAGE MANAGER/CLERK
       ARIMANOVA – critic

14.    SASHA RYUKHIN – committee member
       JUDAS OF KARIOTH – informer
       MSTISLAV LAVROVICH – critic
       BYSTANDER/AUDIENCE MEMBER

15.    MARGARITA
       SINGER

The action takes place on a floor area and three ascending
Constructivist-style stages, linked by flights of steps. "A" is the
highest and smallest stage; "B" is the middle stage; "C" is the
lowest and largest. The floor area is "D".  The costumes are
simple and uniform. Unless otherwise stated, the men wear
grey trousers, grey jackets buttoned to the top and grey flat
caps; the women wear grey skirts, grey jackets and grey head-
scarves. Underwear is grey.

*Satan's Ball* was first performed by the University of Bradford Drama Group at the Edinburgh Festival Fringe 1977, directed and designed by Faynia Williams, music by Phil Wharton.

It won a Scotsman Fringe First for Most Enterprising New Production and was nominated Best Director/Designer, London Critics Awards. It was revived at the University of California Davis, directed and designed by Faynia Williams, in November 1984.

# ACT ONE

*Light discovers three SINGERS, in red tabards, on A, B and C. They sing.*

## THE TOWER OF STATE

A SINGER: Arise –

B SINGER: Work –

C SINGER: Build –

ALL THREE: the Tower of State!
    Live, learn, thrive –
    Man the Master of his Fate!
    All collective, all as one,
    march the People's Army on!
    Iron-muscled, iron-willed –
    Arise, work, build!

*Light discovers the COMPANY in biomechanics poses, ranged from A to D. All wear red tabards.*

COMPANY: Arise, work, build
    the Tower of State!
    Live, learn, thrive –
    Man the Master of his Fate!
    All collective, all as one,
    march the People's Army on!
    Iron-muscled, iron-willed –
    Arise, work, build!

SINGER: From the heat of the battle
    as the red blood flowed,
    from the sweat of the struggle
    to shed our weary load,
    from the teeth of despair,
    from the roar of the gun –

COMPANY: We rose, we laboured, we won!
    Arise, work, build… *(etc.)*

SINGER: *(Over the chorus.)*

But beware brother builders
of evil schemes,
of temples of fanciful
and superstitious dreams!
Renounce where revisionist
and backslider lurk.
The word, brother builders, is Work!

COMPANY: Arise, work, build
the Tower of State!
Live, learn, thrive –
Man the Master of his Fate!

*Company descend to D.*

All collective, all as one,
march the People's Army on!
Iron-muscled, iron-willed –
Arise, work, build!

*Blackout.*

*Light discovers BERLIOZ and BEZDOMNY seated on a block on D. BEZDOMNY has a bundle of scrawled manuscript.*

BEZDOMNY: *(Excited.)* I'm writing a play debunking Jesus Christ! What do you think of it – the idea that Christ was insane? It came to me in a flash! I can't sleep for thinking about it. All my writing up to now has been a preparation for this. But I *have* to have your approval. I couldn't proceed without being a hundred percent sure that every angle, every inference, is grounded in officially acceptable thinking. I feel if I went ahead with it, if I poured my whole *life* into it, and you turned round and said: No, it's not what we want – I'd kill myself!

*He bursts into tears, recovers immediately.*

I've made a few notes. *(Thumbs through pile.)* I'd like you to have a look at them. Tell me what you think. It's just a string of ideas, basic situations. You see I've drawn a parallel between the Roman Principate and our own system of government. I call it the Principate and not the

172

Empire, because the word 'empire' has evil connotations which weren't at all in evidence in the first part of the first century AD. It was a people's government, *for* the people, *by* the people. For instance, Roman citizens were like party members, and the Princeps Augustus, who is dead in the play, but lives on in the hearts and minds of the citizens, parallels our own beloved Comrade Lenin, who is dead in real life but lives on in the welding of the state structure. There's a popular misconception you see, put about by two thousand years of malicious Christian thinking, that the early Roman Principate was brutal, hedonistic, anti-democratic. In fact it was totally the reverse, and was only brutalized *later* by the self-seeking individualism of revisionists like Caligula, Messalina and Nero...

*He continues talking and leafing through notes, as the hooded figure of WOLAND appears on A. BERLIOZ suffers a brief, intense heart attack, accompanied by sudden violent music. BERLIOZ recovers as the figure fades.*

... The warning that I'm spelling out, and I think you'll find it's clear even in note form, is that this descent into complacent brutalism could happen to *us*, if we don't aid the State and perpetuate a concrete faith in the permanence of our glorious system, expelling backsliders and crushing idiot God-fearing pseudo-intellectuals like Jesus Christ and his ilk..

*He continues talking in silence. BERLIOZ addresses the audience.*

BERLIOZ: I am the Chairman of the Writers' Union. I come here every Friday to discuss new ideas with our younger members, and to lend them the benefit of my considerable experience as a bulwark of state culture. I used to anticipate this duty with fervour, but of late I have found that my cardiac condition will not permit me to throw my full weight into their fledgling endeavours. It disturbs me. I can't concentrate. I am beset with nagging fears that my usefulness may be limited, and that if the Bulwark should crumble, the solidity of the Tower itself might be jeopardized...

BEZDOMNY: I don't mind if you don't read it now. I'd like you to take your time. I'd be honoured, Mikhail Alexandrovich, if you considered it was worth serious and detailed examination... *(Continues in silence.)*

BERLIOZ: *(Aside.)* Fortunately I am still robust enough to disguise my debility, and I wish it to be known that I shall continue in my duty for as long as it pleases my inadequate organ to support me...

BEZDOMNY: The central character is Pontius Pilate, Procurator of Judea...

*Light creeps up on PILATE seated on B. He wears a white toga edged with red. His SECRETARY stands beside him in a white tunic, with wax tablet, stilus and sheaf of parchment. There is a vase of red roses.*

*(Continuing.)* ... He's a man of intelligence, a senior servant of the state, a champion of the Stoic philosophy which underlies the Roman structure; but he's cramped by the bigotry of the Jews, by the lack of intellectual stimulus and by chronic migraine. He is interviewing a prisoner from Galilee...

*Light fades on D as the SECRETARY and PILATE speak. YESHUA HA-NOTSRI, on C, in grey ragged robe, hands bound behind him, stands before PILATE, guarded by the centurion MARK MURIBELLUM.*

SECRETARY: *(Handing parchment to PILATE.)* The prisoner from Galilee sir.

PILATE: What is he doing here?

SECRETARY: The Sanhedrin has passed a death sentence which has to be confirmed by you sir.

PILATE: Not if he comes from Galilee. It's the Tetrarch's business, not mine.

SECRETARY: The case has been before the Tetrarch sir and he has declined to confirm the Sanhedrin's findings.

PILATE: Why?

SECRETARY: I imagine he is anxious not to put a foot wrong sir.

PILATE: He's a coward.

YESHUA: Cowardice is the greatest sin, good man.

MURIBELLUM: Speak when you're spoken to!

PILATE: Name? Name!

YESHUA: My name?

MURIBELLUM: He knows his own name.

PILATE: Muribellum –

MURIBELLUM: Sir.

YESHUA: Yeshua.

PILATE: Surname.

YESHUA: Ha-Notsri.

PILATE: Where are you from?

YESHUA: Galilee.

PILATE: Who are you by birth?

YESHUA: I don't know exactly –

PILATE: Where is your fixed abode?

YESHUA: I have no fixed abode.

MURIBELLUM: He's a vagrant sir.

PILATE: He's an idiot.

YESHUA: Blessed is the fool, for he shall inherit the earth!

MURIBELLUM: Is he wasting your time sir?

PILATE: Do you know who I am?

YESHUA: You are a good man.

PILATE: Am I?

YESHUA: As are all men, good man, and you are no
     exception. There are no evil people on earth.

PILATE: Muribellum.

MURIBELLUM: Sir?

PILATE: Teach him how to address me.

MURIBELLUM: Sir.

PILATE: Then bring him back.

MURIBELLUM: Sir.

PILATE: Don't mutilate him.

MURIBELLUM: I'll try not to sir.

*He forces YESHUA to his knees and prepares to flog him. PILATE's head is splitting.*

SECRETARY: Are you all right sir?

PILATE: Stench of roses...

SECRETARY: They alleviate the smell of the city sir.

PILATE: They drill through my brain.

SECRETARY: Hemicrania sir? Shall I fetch a doctor?

PILATE: There's no cure.

SECRETARY: You need an anodyne balsam sir.

PILATE: I need poison...

MURIBELLUM: You call him *sir*! *(Crack!)*

YESHUA: Aaaaaargh!

MURIBELLUM: Understand? *(Crack!)*

YESHUA: Aaaaaargh!

MURIBELLUM: He's not a good man, he's not a nice man, he's not a kind man... *(Crack!)*

YESHUA: Aaaaaargh!

MURIBELLUM: He's a raving monster like me!

PILATE: I hate this place. I hate these idiot people, the noise, the heat, the stench...

SECRETARY: You need a holiday sir. You're over-zealous in the execution of your duties. Hemicrania graduates from stress.

*MURIBELLUM helps YESHUA to his knees. Pause. PILATE consults parchment.*

PILATE: You have incited the people to destroy the temple building.

YESHUA: No sir.

PILATE: Isn't that a senseless thing to do?

YESHUA: Yes sir.

PILATE: Why did you do it?

YESHUA: I didn't – sir.

PILATE: It says here that you did.

YESHUA: It's wrong.

PILATE: It is written!

YESHUA: It is wrong.

PILATE: There are witnesses. You made a speech. You said:
Tear down the temple –

YESHUA: I spoke of the temple of the old beliefs –

PILATE: I don't care which precise words you used. The
impression you created was one of incitement to civil
disruption.

YESHUA: I used the word "temple" to mean –

PILATE: Now *I* wouldn't care one *fig* if you engineered the
complete removal of this garbage-tip. I'd probably rejoice!
But the fact remains that I am responsible for law and
order among your excitable people, even when wide-eyed
dreamers such as yourself oblige me by going around
advocating the demolition of your hideous national
monuments – *(To SECRETARY.)* Do you have to write down
everything I say?

SECRETARY: It's to your advantage in the long run sir.

PILATE: Strike it out.

SECRETARY: I'll make a note that you wish...

PILATE: Strike it out.

SECRETARY: ...this passage to be struck out.

PILATE: I don't wish this interview to be recorded.

SECRETARY: *(Writing.)* ...to be recorded.

   *Pause.*

YESHUA: I have that trouble too. Wherever I go, there's a man
who follows me, taking down everything I say.

SECRETARY: It goes against the usual practice sir.

PILATE: Close the book.

SECRETARY: With your permission sir –

PILATE: Close it!

YESHUA: The difference in my case is that he generally gets it wrong. He elaborates. I once caught a glimpse of what he was writing. *(Laughs.)* He said I fed 5000 people. He said I walked on water. He said I cleansed lepers and raised the dead! His name is Matthew. He's a Levite, a tax-collector. I met him on the road to Bethphagy, at the corner where the road passes a fig orchard. I started talking to him. He was rude. He even insulted me – or thought he was insulting me. He called me a dog. Personally I like dogs, as you do, so I wasn't offended. I talked on well into the evening, and he listened. He made notes and heard me out, and in the end, he threw his money in the road and said he would go travelling with me.

MURIBELLUM: *(Laughing.)* A tax-collector throwing his money away!

YESHUA: He's followed me ever since. *(Pause.)*

PILATE: You made a speech about the Temple. What exactly did you say?

YESHUA: I said the temple of the old beliefs would fall down and a new temple of truth would be built up.

PILATE: What truth is this?

YESHUA: The truth of your head-ache… which has now gone… *(Smiles.)* It's clear. You can look at me. The simple truth that you are a good man.

PILATE: Untie his hands.

MURIBELLUM: Sir?

*MURIBELLUM unties YESHUA's hands.*

YESHUA: You should take a walk. Breathe some fresh air. Your life is cramped. You're a man of great intelligence, sensitive to truth, but your mind is closed. You're dangerously close to losing your faith in human beings. Your only friend is your dog, but he can't talk. *(Pause.)* There are several things I'd like to discuss with you, away from this cramped place…

PILATE: You maintain that you never incited people to tear down or burn or by any means demolish the Temple?

YESHUA: I have never tried to persuade anyone to attempt to do any such thing.

PILATE: Good.

YESHUA: It would be senseless, not to say impossible.

PILATE: Do you happen to know a political activist called Dismas?

YESHUA: No.

PILATE: Hestus?

YESHUA: No.

PILATE: Bar-Abba?

YESHUA: No.

PILATE: Good.

SECRETARY: *(Showing him in the parchment.)* There is one further charge sir.

PILATE: I have examined you and I find no grounds for confirming your sentence.

SECRETARY: The charge of treason sir. It is stated here that he spoke out against Caesar. *(PILATE takes the document.)* The witness is one Judas of Karioth.

PILATE: *(To YESHUA.)* Do you know him?

YESHUA: Yes.

PILATE: Is he a "good man"?

YESHUA: Yes.

PILATE: He trapped you.

YESHUA: He is a very good man. He expressed great interest in my ideas. He invited me to his home. He gave me supper. He asked me my views on government. The question seemed to interest him very much.

PILATE: What did you say? *(To SECRETARY.)* Note this.

*The SECRETARY takes notes. PILATE's head-ache returns.*

YESHUA: I said all power is a form of violence exercised over people. The time will come when there will be no rule by Caesar, nor any other form of rule. Man will pass into the Kingdom of Justice and Truth, where no sort of power will be needed.

PILATE: Ye gods...

YESHUA: Then some men in ran and tied me up and took me to prison. *(Pause.)* I have spoken the truth.

PILATE: Bind him.

YESHUA: Let me go! *(MURIBELLUM binds him.)*

PILATE: Do you believe in the gods?

YESHUA: God is One.

PILATE: Then pray to him.

YESHUA: Lord Lord save this good man –

PILATE: *(Stands.)* Is that how you seen the Principate?

YESHUA: Save him from his greatest sin!

*MURIBELLUM drags YESHUA back to C.*

PILATE: Is that how you regard the struggle and sacrifice of the Roman people to bring peace to the world? The Principate was born from the blood of men who believed in a structured future for mankind! The Roman power is the power of *service*! We have no perverted desire to swat you like flies. We give you stability, justice, peace! It's yours! It's for all the people!

YESHUA: God save you good man.

PILATE: Take him away.

MURIBELLUM: *(Salutes.)* Hail Caesar!

*MURIBELLUM drags YESHUA away.*

PILATE: It creeps up, behind the eye. It drills through: an iron wedge, a clot of pain...

SECRETARY: Sir?

PILATE: Shut out the light.

*Cross-fade to D. BERLIOZ and BEZDOMNY as before.*

BEZDOMNY: You don't like it.

BERLIOZ: Your Christ is alive.

BEZDOMNY: He dies.

BERLIOZ: You establish that he lived.

BEZDOMNY: He did!

BERLIOZ: Proof.

BEZDOMNY: It's written.

BERLIOZ: By whom? The gospels are a pack of lies. You've said so. The reliable historians of the period don't mention him.

BEZDOMNY: Tacitus Annals book 15.

BERLIOZ: A forgery. Christ was invented. That must be the theme of your play.

BEZDOMNY: He has to be there! We have to see him!

BERLIOZ: You're writing lies.

BEZDOMNY: I'm honing down the Christ phenomenon to its basic essentials, to show that there is no substance for the building of a moralistic religion.

BERLIOZ: There is no substance because there was no Christ.

BEZDOMNY: That's not the point.

BERLIOZ: It's the only point and you must prove it.

BEZDOMNY: This is a play, not a thesis!

BERLIOZ: He was concocted by the Christians.

BEZDOMNY: I have to establish that there was a man –

BERLIOZ: Just as other religions have always concocted virgin-born gods when it suited them.

BEZDOMNY: I don't mention his birth.

BERLIOZ: You don't deny it.

BEZDOMNY: You don't understand what I'm doing –

*WOLAND has descended from A during their argument. He wears a long black overcoat, beret and long red scarf.*

BERLIOZ: Name me one eastern religion, that doesn't induce an immaculate virgin to sprout a son of God. They were all at it. It was obviously convenient for the perpetuation of ignorance among the proletariat.

WOLAND: May I join you? *(Descends to D.)* Do continue...

BERLIOZ: Christ was a carbon copy of Osiris, Dionysus, Mithras –

WOLAND: ...Adonis, Tammuz, Attis, Marduk, Vitzli-Putzli – he was an Aztec. They used to model figurines of him out of dough.

BEZDOMNY: I'll burn it.

BERLIOZ: Rewrite it.

WOLAND: Destroy the manuscript and you destroy the man. Forgive me, I'm intruding. You were saying that Christ never existed.

BERLIOZ: That is right.

WOLAND: *(To BEZDOMNY.)* Do you agree?

BEZDOMNY: I believe that the founder of the Christian religion was insane.

WOLAND: Is that so bad?

BEZDOMNMY: It's a fact.

WOLAND: Are you an atheist?

BEZDOMNY: We don't believe in God.

WOLAND: How extraordinary!

BERLIOZ: There's nothing irregular about atheism.

BEZDOMNY: We believe in man.

WOLAND: What does God say to that?

BERLIOZ: There is no rational proof of the existence of God.

WOLAND: How do you account for his presence?

BEZDOMNY: We've abolished fairy tales.

WOLAND: Don't talk so loud.

BERLIOZ: It may be sir, that where you come from, society has not yet reached that level of maturity –

WOLAND: Who rules the life of man and keeps the world in order?

BEZDOMNY: Man rules himself.

WOLAND: But to rule, one must have a precise plan.

BERLIOZ: We have an intricate network of precise plans.

WOLAND: Amazing!

BEZDOMNY: We organize our affairs –

WOLAND: For how long? A thousand years? Ten minutes? Two seconds? How can you *know* what will happen tomorrow? I'm really interested.

BERLIOZ: Of course, we can't be one hundred percent certain –

WOLAND: …that the old ticker won't play up? Yes I understand.

BERLIOZ: We have contingency plans, deputies to step in. It's all arranged.

WOLAND: But what happens to *you* when the clock runs away with itself? Suddenly you're unreliable! Suddenly all that interests you is *you*! The plan goes by the board. Your principles evaporate. You rush to the doctor, then to the specialist, then to the faith-healer, then to the fortune-teller. You're guilty, you're mad, you're out of control, you're *religious*!

BERLIOZ: Of course man is mortal –

WOLAND: And mortality has a cunning way of creeping up on you…

*Pause.*

BERLIOZ: *(Rising.)* I have a meeting.

WOLAND: What makes you say that?

BERLIOZ: Will you excuse me now?

WOLAND: What makes you think you have a meeting?

BERLIOZ: It is in my diary.

WOLAND: Can you swear that at seven o'clock this evening, you will take the chair at the Executive Committee of the Writers' Union?

BEZDOMNY: *(Amazed.)* How did you know…?

WOLAND: How can man control his own affairs when he is incapable of predicting what will happen this evening?

BERLIOZ: I will be there.

WOLAND: No you won't.

BEZDOMNY: You can't detain him.

BERLIOZ: Provided a brick doesn't land on me.

WOLAND: It won't be a brick.

BERLIOZ: Provided my heart –

WOLAND: Your heart is fine. It will serve you well for the rest of your life.

BEZDOMNY: Look excuse me, but I think we've had enough –

BERLIOZ: How will I die?

WOLAND: Frightened?

BERLIOZ: Not in the least.

BEZDOMNY: Comrade Berlioz is a pillar of the state. He has no fears of the unknown. He leads a constructive and temperate life. He's an example to us all. I only wish I had his confidence, his insight, his honesty, his moral strength, his ability to analyse. It's because I trust him that I can take his criticism. I can accept his rejection of my work, because I know his motives are soundly based. He's the driving force behind my creativity –

WOLAND: Your head will be cut off, by a woman. You won't feel a thing. Anna has already bought the sunflower oil. She has tripped. She has already spilt it. *(Smiles.)* You won't make your committee meeting tonight. *(Pause.)*

BERLIOZ: How long sir have you been in Moscow?

WOLAND: I've just arrived.

BERLIOZ: Have you come here alone?

WOLAND: I'm expecting some friends.

BERLIOZ: Where are you staying?

WOLAND: In your apartment.

BEZDOMNY: He's mad!

WOLAND: As mad as Christ?

BERLIOZ: I'm afraid you won't be very comfortable.

WOLAND: You won't be there.

BEZDOMNY: May we see your papers? *(Pause.)*

WOLAND: Ah… *(Taps his pockets.)* Forgive me…

BEZDOMNY: *(To BERLIOZ.)* He has no papers! Arrest him!

WOLAND: *(Producing papers as if by magic.)* I never introduced myself: Professor Woland. Passport, visa, union card, medical certificate, and I have a letter inviting me to Moscow for consultations.

BERLIOZ: What is your particular field of work?

WOLAND: Black magic.

BEZDOMNY: He's a spy!

BERLIOZ: *(To WOLAND.)* Would you like to see the city?

WOLAND: I'd be delighted.

BERLIOZ: Perhaps you'd care to wait here a moment with Comrade Bezdomny, while I telephone the Tourist Board for a guide. I'd gladly show you the sights myself –

WOLAND: But you have a meeting!

BERLIOZ: And Comrade Bezdomny –

WOLAND: …has an appointment with Pontius Pilate.

BERLIOZ: Exactly.

WOLAND: *(Bows.)* You're most kind.

BERLIOZ: Au revoir.

WOLAND: Adieu.

*BERLIOZ moves away.*

*(To BEZDOMNY.)* Does Christ get off? Which way does Pilate choose? I'm fascinated.

BEZDOMNY: *(Nervous.)* He has to follow the official line. He has to act for the state.

WOLAND: There's a loop-hole. See if he finds it.

*Cross-fade to BERLIOZ solo.*

BERLIOZ: My plan is simple. I shall cross the road and run to the nearest telephone box, to contact the Aliens' Bureau… *(Sound of traffic.)* …I shall tell them there is a foreign professor newly arrived in the city, who is clearly insane, and a potential menace to society… *(Sound of a tram approaching at speed.)* …I shall use my authority to demand his immediate arrest for questioning –

*Blackout as WOMAN screams and tram brakes screech. Immediate cut to BEZDOMNY solo, his face a gaping mask of horror. Voices of BYSTANDERS softly in the shadows.*

1 BYSTANDER: He fell on the track…

2 BYSTANDER: It was Anna. She was carrying a jug of sunflower oil…

1 BYSTANDER: It came straight at him. It wouldn't stop…

2 BYSTANDER: She was laughing, she tripped…

3 BYSTANDER: The tram-driver's in a terrible state…

4 BYSTANDER: He must have slipped on the oil…

3 BYSTANDER: It was her first day. She's never driven on her own before…

2 BYSTANDER: It passed right over him. He disappeared…

3 BYSTANDER: It wasn't her fault. She couldn't see…

4 BYSTANDER: His head was cut off by the wheels!

*Cross-fade to PILATE and SECRETARY on B.*

SECRETARY: Sir.

PILATE: What is it?

SECRETARY: There's a loop-hole. The mad preacher may yet be released.

PILATE: He is condemned. I have confirmed it. In half an hour, I have to appear before the multitude to pronounce sentence.

SECRETARY: According to local custom sir, you may also pronounce which prisoner is to be freed. In honour of the Passover, one prisoner by tradition, may be released. Naturally, the Sanhedrin should be consulted. This clemency, for political reasons, should accord with their advice.

PILATE: How many prisoners are there?

SECRETARY: Four sir: Dismas, Hestus, Bar-Abba and Ha-Notsri. I am sure, with a few carefully chosen words sir, you could persuade the High Priest to recommend Ha-Notsri. I can see how his case has affected you sir.

PILATE: He is insane.

SECRETARY: He seems to have the power to cure your head-ache sir.

PILATE: He should be kept away from public places. These people are excitable and he talks too much.

SECRETARY: Might I suggest sir, that should he be released, you incarcerate him loosely in your palace at Caesarea – as your librarian perhaps. I feel it would be to your advantage sir, to have him on hand, as a dialectical sedative, for moments of stress.

PILATE: Fetch Caiaphas.

SECRETARY: Yes sir.

*Cut to BEZDOMNY solo as before.*

BEZDOMNY: I saw the head! It rolled! It bounced! It stared up at me from the cobbles! I bit my hand till it bled! I saw the driver – a woman! And someone said: Anna! She spilt the sunflower oil! He knew it was going to happen!

*As he speaks, light creeps up on C. At the table are seated: HELLA, in long black dress with long red hair, BEHEMOTH, a vast black cat with red eyes, smoking a cigar, and AZAZELLO, a boy in a black and red check suit and cap.*

*(Continuing.)* I ran back to where we were sitting. He wasn't there. Instead, there was a woman in black with bright red hair, a boy in a check suit, and a cat, the size of a pig! Smoking a cigar! As I approached them, they *vanished*!

*His light snaps out.*

HELLA: *(To BEHEMOTH.)* Did he instruct you to come like that?

BEHEMOTH: Like what?

HELLA: I think you should change.

BEHEMOTH: I think you should shaddap.

AZAZELLO: *(Sniffing the air.)* Are you *sure* this is the right place? It's so evil…

HELLA: His implicit instructions were that we should come as ordinary persons.

AZAZELLO: So corrupt, so drab…

HELLA: Azazello and I have sacrificed a great deal to fall in with his stipulations. We feel it is most unfair for you to retain your trappings while we suffer the limitations of the human frame.

AZAZELLO: You can smell it: the melancholia, the dullness…

HELLA: The poor boy has given up his tail, his wings, his horns, his cloven feet; and I myself have been obliged to forfeit two of my three heads.

BEHEMOTH: You'll have to stop talking to yourself then won't you?

AZAZELLO: The place reeks! There's nothing left for us to *do*!

BEHEMOTH: I wasn't intending to do anything.

HELLA: Lazy feline slob!

AZAZELLO: We've been here half an hour. There's not been one *whiff* of enterprise!

BEHEMOTH: I shall curl up and fart.

AZAZELLO: It's foul. It's rotten…

HELLA: I should have thought if you were intending to come in your "pussy" persona, you'd at least have appeared as the average cat in the street.

BEHEMOTH: *(Farts.)*

HELLA: It's ridiculous. You won't fool anyone. You're as big as a pig!

AZAZELLO: I'd been led to believe that this place was a shining temple of light, thronging with energetic, virtuous, highly sensitive, truth-seeking souls! The Perfect State! Purity, beauty, passion, art!

BEHEMOTH: You've got a lot to learn son.

HELLA: Let's leave the philosophizing to Himself shall we?

AZAZELLO: Let me get this straight. The purpose of the Ball is to crush.

HELLA: Is this your first time love?

AZAZELLO: Satan comes up with his retinue to dance on the souls of the Enlightened, and drain their aspirations, quench their passions –

HELLA: I have attended a fair number of Satan's Balls – he likes me to be there. I have a uniquely depressing effect.

AZAZELLO: So where are they – the truth-seekers?

BEHEMOTH: Relax son.

AZAZELLO: Whom can we squash?

BEHEMOTH: Just relish the odium of the moment.

HELLA: I have learnt that one must do as one is instructed, and never raise questions.

BEHEMOTH: She thinks she's going to be hostess.

HELLA: He has hinted as much. After centuries of torment, he has finally succumbed to my guiles…

BEHEMOTH: She always says that.

HELLA: Our union shall be fused.

BEHEMOTH: She never gets him.

HELLA: I shall sing for him tomorrow night!

BEHEMOTH: That's why she's so depressing.

AZAZELLO: There's been a mistake. We've come to the wrong place. It's a trick!

*WOLAND appears through the table in a puff of smoke.*

WOLAND: It's a whole *bag* of tricks boy!

AZAZELLO: Sir –

BEHEMOTH: Boss –

HELLA: Messire!

WOLAND: Brace yourselves fiends, for the shock of the purpose of our mission!

AZAZELLO: We're ready!

BEHEMOTH: What is it?

HELLA: Tell us tell us!

WOLAND: You won't like it.

AZAZELLO: Oh we will!

BEHEMOTH: We'll love it!

HELLA: We'll adore it!

WOLAND: We are here, in Moscow, indirectly, in the cause of Good.

BEHEMOTH: God's Piss!

AZAZELLO: Holy Jobs!

HELLA: Dung of Christ!

WOLAND: *(Leading them to B.)* It is a critical mission and we have to succeed! There is a crust of doom suppressing life in these parts.

HELLA: Surely that is what we want!

BEHEMOTH: Total evil!

WOLAND: If we fail, the word Evil will be expunged from the vocabulary of man.

AZAZELLO: Hell's balls!

WOLAND: We have done too well. Evil rules!

BEHEMOTH: That's right!

HELLA: But but but –

AZAZELLO: By Evil, do you mean fear, corruption, malice, deceit, apathy, spite, cowardice – ?

WOLAND: All these evils have merged to form a barrier through which Good has no chance of escape!

BEHEMOTH: That's right!

HELLA: But but but –

AZAZELLO: By Good do you mean courage, ambition, inspiration, passion, integrity – ?

WOLAND: We have to crack this barrier to let the Good fly out!

BEHEMOTH: It's against our nature.

WOLAND: It's basic economics! If Good is extinguished, Evil no longer has meaning. There has to be a contest! We are here to resurrect that contest before it is too late!!

*Cut to BEZDOMNY solo.*

BEZDOMNY: How did he know about Pilate? Why did he twist my thoughts? There are no loopholes in the perfect state! Christ was mad! He discredited the rule of law! He cannot be released! Pilate will not allow it!

*Cut to the table on C around which are seated the Executive Committee of the Writers' Union: ARCHIBALD ARCHIBALDOVICH, SASHA RYUKHIN and NASTASYA LUKINISHNA.*

ARCHIBALD: How long have we been waiting?

RYUKHIN: Three hours.

NASTASYA: We should press on with the meeting. We have urgent business. Dissident writers are promoting their work abroad, slandering the state, and earning for themselves obscene wads of illegal foreign currency. As Executive Committee of the Writers' Union, it is our duty to stamp them out!

ARCHIBALD: We cannot proceed without our Chairman.

RYUKHIN: It's most unlike him. He's always so punctual...

*Cut to BEZDOMNY.*

BEZDOMNY: I saw them!

*Light comes up on B as WOLAND leads his RETINUE in slow silhouetted demonic song and dance.*

## WITHOUT JOY

WOLAND: Without joy
    there is no grief.
    You can't shatter the man
    with no belief.
    You can't blind the eyes
    and tear the face
    if the face ain't there
    in the first place.

BEZDOMNY: The professor, the boy, the woman and the cat.
    They turned a corner down an alley…

WOLAND: *(Leads them dancing to B.)*
    Without a sail
    there is no wreck.
    You can't strangle the man
    who has no neck.
    You can't spill high hopes
    and spread regret
    if the will to live
    ain't alive yet.

BEZDOMNY: I ran after them. I had to catch them, turn them
    over to the police. The alley was dark. I heard whispers.

WOLAND: *(Leads them dancing to A.)*
    Without a smile
    there is no frown.
    If birds don't fly
    you can't shoot them down.
    If none can aspire
    none can fall
    and there ain't no Satan's

Ball at all

*DEVILS fade. BEZDOMNY alone.*

BEZDOMNY: A light appeared. A window opened. A woman yelled at me to go away. They'd gone…

*Cross-fade to the table. TAMARA POLUMESYATZ has joined the committee members.*

TAMARA: He was beheaded by a tram.

NASTASYA: So that's his excuse!

TAMARA: They took him to the morgue and laid him out on three tables. I got the details from the pathologist.

ARCHIBALD: Such a terrible loss.

RYUKHIN: Such cruelty. Such violence.

NASTASYA: We must show that we can cope.

TAMARA: On the first table was his naked, blood-caked body with a fractured arm and a smashed rib-cage. On the second was his head with its teeth knocked in and the eyes glaring up at the blinding light. And on the third, was a heap of mangled rags.

ARCHIBALD: He was a pillar of the state.

RYUKHIN: An example to us all.

NASTASYA: We should respect his memory and soldier on with the meeting.

TAMARA: They couldn't decide whether to sew the head back on, or just cover him over with a black cloth.

NASTASYA: He would have wished for a senior committee member to deputize as Chairman. We have a responsibility to our members. We have to regulate writers who are stepping out of line.

TAMARA: Comrade Bezdomny was with him. He saw the accident.

*Cross-fade to BEZDOMNY in undershorts, crouched on the block in D.*

BEZDOMNY: I have to clear my brain. I have to wash out the ghosts that tug at me. The state is good. Christ cannot be spared. We cannot permit loop-holes. Evil forces must be stopped before they eat through the structure of my life…

*Cross-fade to the table.*

TAMARA: He stripped off his clothes and took a dive into the river.

RYUKHIN: Suicide!

NASTASYA: We've abolished suicide.

TAMARA: When he got out, he couldn't find his clothes. He was last seen running down back alleys, dripping wet in his undershorts, yelling for the police to arrest a foreign professor.

NASTASYA: Let's hope he's taken care of.

ARCHIBALD: Where is he now?

TAMARA: We don't know.

RYUKHIN: He might come here. He's a member.

NASTASYA: Not without his card.

ARCHIBALD: Unless he keeps it in his undershorts!

NASTASYA: He has applied for a grant. What do we know about him Archibald Archibaldovich?

ARCHIBALD: *(Consulting file.)* Um…er… age twenty-three, hair dark, eyes grey, height five foot seven…

RYUKHIN: There's a compulsive energy in his writing.

NASTASYA: Is that written down?

RYUKHIN: I've read his work.

NASTASYA: Let's stick to what's in the file.

ARCHIBALD: *(Reading.)* Short-sighted, asthmatic, neurasthenic, insomniac…

NASTASYA: Do we put him forward for scrutiny?

TAMARA:  I don't think so.

ARCHIBALD: Not on today's showing.

NASTASYA: *(To RYUKHIN.)* Comrade?

RYUKHIN: Er… no.

NASTASYA: Strike him off.

*ARCHIBALD strikes him off. They move on to further business.*

RYUKHIN: *(Aside.)* I'm a coward. Bezdomny is my friend. He's in a bad way. He needs that grant. I told him I would speak up for him. It's too late now…

*WOLAND appears in white jacket and chef's hat.*

TAMARA: Comrades, owing to the lateness of the hour, the pressure of business, and the need to keep our spirits keen and our bodies whole, in the face of today's appalling tragedy –

ARCHIBALD: Terrible.

NASTASYA: We must be firm.

TAMARA: I move that we order supper.

ARCHIBALD: Seconded.

NASTASYA: I move that we continue the business through supper.

TAMARA: Seconded.

NASTASYA: Let's have the menu.

WOLAND: Filleted sturgeon with lobsters' tails and fresh caviare –

ARCHIBALD: Thank you.

WOLAND: *Oeufs en cocotte* with mushroom purée –

TAMARA: Thank you.

WOLAND: *Quails alla Genovese* –

RYUKHIN: Thank you.

WOLAND: And thrushes' breasts with truffles.

NASTASYA: Thank you.

TAMARA: I move that we compliment Archibald Archibaldovich upon his excellent supervision of the cuisine.

ARCHIBALD: You haven't tasted it yet!

TAMARA: Sheer virtuosity, and so reasonable, at eight roubles fifty.

NASTASYA: Committee privilege.

ARCHIBALD: Justly deserved.

TAMARA: Such a pity our chairman isn't here to appreciate it.

ARCHIBALD: Tragic! Appalling!

NASTASYA: We have to live on!

RYUKHIN: *(Aside.)* I'm not hungry. I hate quails. I resent committee privileges, but I daren't speak out. I disgust myself...

*WOLAND appears with AZAZELLO, HELLA and BEHEMOTH, in white coats as waiters. They serve the suppers.*

NASTASYA: We have to consider the question of certain members and ex-members promoting their work abroad –

ARCHIBALD: *(Receiving sturgeon from AZAZELLO.)* Thank you.

NASTASYA: We have information of malicious lies ridiculing and vilifying the control of culture –

TAMARA: *(Receiving oeufs en cocotte from HELLA.)* Thank you.

NASTASYA: ...concocting rumours of corruption and indulgence in our institutions –

RYUKHIN: *(Receiving quails from WOLAND.)* Thank you.

NASTASYA: ...and slandering the committee structure with allegations that palms are being greased and pockets lined with a steady influx – *(Receives thrushes' breasts from BEHEMOTH.)* Thank you – of prohibited foreign currency...

*AZAZELLO whispers to ARCHIBALD as they eat.*

ARCHIBALD: You what...? I beg your pardon...?

TAMARA: What's he saying?

ARCHIBALD: He's saying if it's all right by us, he'll accept his tip tonight in dollars!

TAMARA: The cheek!

NASTASYA: Is this a joke?

AZAZELLO: *(Whispers.)*

ARCHIBALD: He says he knows our pockets are stuffed with them, and for a consideration –

TAMARA: I'll give him consideration!

NASTASYA: I've never seen you before. Where are you from?

*BEZDOMNY bursts in soaking wet in his undershorts.*

BEZDOMNY: It's *him*!

RYUKHIN: Ivan Nikolayich!

BEZDOMNY: Stop them! It's the professor! I was there! I saw it!

ARCHIBALD: *(Restraining him.)* Steady boy –

BEZDOMNY: He killed Mikhail Alexandrovich!

NASTASYA: Now just a minute –

BEZDOMNY: The cat!!

TAMARA: What cat?

BEZDOMNY: *There!*

NASTASYA: He's drunk!

*In the confusion WOLAND and RETINUE have disappeared taking the suppers.*

BEZDOMNY: Call the police! Tell them to bring machine-guns!

NASTASYA: Hold him! We can't allow this.

ARCHIBALD: Whoa boy! Steady!

BEZDOMNY: *(Breaking loose.)* He'll kill you all! He'll sabotage the state! He advocated the liberation of Christ!

NASTASYA: Call a psychiatrist.

BEZDOMNY: Get off me you bureaucratic bitch! You're all the same! You're frauds!

RYUKHIN: You're clearly upset by the death of our beloved Mikhail Alexandrovich –

BEZDOMNY: *(Attacking him.)* Who do you think you *are*?

RYUKHIN: It's all right Vanya…

BEZDOMNY: You haven't written a word of truth in your life! You churn it out! You're a machine! "Onwards and

Upwards!", "Banners Waving!", "Arise Work Build!" It's false! It's not what you're thinking up here! You're told to do it and you do it by numbers! It's not *you*!

*A POLICE OFFICER arrests BEZDOMNY.*

OFFICER: Will you come quietly sir?

BEZDOMNY: They're coming for you! They'll get you! The forces of evil will crush the state! They can only be stopped by the *truth*!

*He is dragged away, given a grey dressing-gown and confined to the block in D. Bars are raised at either end of it.*

*ARCHIBALD gives RYUKHIN money.*

ARCHIBALD: Here. Run after him. See that he's properly looked after.

TANARA: Disgusting! Appalling!

NASTASYA: He'll never get his grant.

ARCHIBALD: *(To RYUKHIN.)* What's the matter man? What are you waiting for?

RYUKHIN: *(Looking at the money.)* You gave me dollars?

NASTASYA: Dollars?

RYUKHIN: Foreign currency.

*Wads of dollars are exuding from ARCHIBALD's pockets.*

ARCHIBALD: Merciful heavens! I swear I –

TAMARA: Archibald Archibaldovich is stuffed with dollars!

NASTASYA: This is no joke –

TAMARA: *(Dollars sprouting from her pockets.)* Oh my God!

ARCHIBALD: You too comrade!

TAMARA: Hundreds of them!

RYUKHIN: *(Sprouting dollars.)* Oh hell…

ARCHIBALD: How the devil – ?

NASTASYA: Comrades I fear it is my unpleasant duty –

TAMARA: Feel in your own pockets Nastasya Lukinishna!

NASTASYA: *(Finding wads of dollars.)* What is the meaning of this?

ARCHIBALD: I demand an enquiry!

TAMARA: It's a conspiracy!

ARCHIBALD: A criminal plot to discredit the committee.

TAMARA: I have served for sixteen years!

NASTASYA: Comrades, comrades…

ARCHIBALD: I have a family to support –

TAMARA: I am a buttress of the union –

NASTASYA: Comrades, I feel, in the interests of state security, in the absence of witnesses, for the continued welfare of this committee, it might be politic, under the circumstances, not to divulge…

*They begin to put away the money. Focus on RYUKHIN.*

RYUKHIN: *(Aside.)* This is the punishment for cowardice. Bezdomny was right. I'm a fraud. I don't believe in a single word I've ever written. It's worthless churned-out pulp. I've never dared stand up for what I *think*! I toe the line. And so it goes on…

*They go out, counting their dollars.*

ARCHIBALD: 110, 120, 130…

NASTASYA: 200, 300, 400, 500…

TAMARA: 55, 60, 65, 70, 75…

RYUKHIN: 12, 13, 14, 15…

*Cross-fade to D. BEZDOMNY, seated in his dressing-gown. NURSE PRASKOVYA FYODOROVNA in white coat, comes in briskly.*

NURSE: Good morning! How do we feel this morning? *(Prepares syringe.)* This'll do you good!

BEZDOMNY: Where am I?

NURSE: *(Injecting him.)* You're quite safe here. It's our job to look after you. Make you better. Return you to the world as a normal, nicely-behaved, hard-working human being. All right?

BEZDOMNY: Thank you Nurse.

*Enter DR. STRAVINSKY, in white coat and spectacles. NURSE has a clipboard.*

NURSE: This is Dr Stravinsky.

STRAVINSKY: How are we today?

NURSE: He's a playwright.

STRAVINSKY: *(Inspects him.)* Uh-huh... uh-huh...

BEZDOMNY: Are you a professor?

STRAVINSKY: Uh-huh...

BEZDOMNY: Are you in charge here?

STRAVINSKY: Uh-huh...

BEZDOMNY: I must talk to you.

STRAVINSKY: Splendid!

BEZDOMNY: No one will listen to me.

STRAVINSKY: Why is that I wonder?

BEZDOMNY: They say I'm mad.

STRAVINSKY: Is that so?

BEZDOMNY: Yesterday I met a mysterious person who may or may not have been a foreigner.

STRAVINSKY: I'm listening. *(To NURSE.)* Is he under sedation? *(Confers with her, consulting notes.)*

BEZDOMNY: I was with my friend the Chairman of the Writers' Union.

STRAVINSKY: *(To NURSE.)* Yes...

BEZDOMNY: This man knew about the death of the Chairman before it happened.

STRAVINSKY: Yes, yes...

BEZDOMNY: He told us the details word for word. He said Anna had spilt the sunflower oil. He said the tram-driver was a woman. He knew it all. He told us every detail before it happened!

STRAVINSKY: I see.

BEZDOMNY: Do you understand me?

STRAVINSKY: *(To BEZDOMNY.)* Who is Anna?

BEZDOMNY: That doesn't matter.

STRAVINSKY: Good.

BEZDOMNY: He has a power. He is evil. He must be stopped.

STRAVINSKY: Have you reported this to the police?

BEZDOMNY: No one listens!

STRAVINSKY: Go on.

*NURSE draws his attention to further notes. They confer.*

BEZDOMNY: He has accomplices. There's a woman in black, a boy in a check suit, and a cat, the size of a pig!

STRAVINSKY: *(To BEZDOMNY.)* And you feel he should be arrested?

BEZDOMNY: He's a criminal! He's undermining the fabric of the state. He's hacking away at my commitment as a writer!

STRAVINSKY: How exactly?

BEZDOMNY: He knows about Pontius Pilate.

STRAVINSKY: Is this the Pilate who was Procurator of Judea?

BEZDOMNY: Yes!

STRAVINSKY: What does he know about him? *(Confers with NURSE.)*

BEZDOMNY: He knows that Pilate is looking, against his better judgment, for a loop-hole through which to release Jesus Christ!

STRAVINSKY: That's too bad.

BEZDOMNY: You've got to let me out.

STRAVINSKY: We shall.

BEZDOMNY: *Now!*

STRAVINSKY: It's no problem. We shall let you out, quite freely, with no conditions, to go on with your daily life exactly as you wish, just as soon as you tell me that you are normal.

BEZDOMNY: I am normal.

STRAVINSKY: Splendid.

BEZDOMNY: May I go?

STRAVINSKY: Let's be logical.

BEZDOMNY: I'm normal!

STRAVINSKY: Yesterday, a man whom you admire, was killed suddenly. You had reason to believe that a certain stranger was criminally involved in his death, and you set about securing his arrest. You maintain that he foretold the circumstances of your friend's death, that he had accomplices – two human and one feline – and that he knew the thoughts of Pontius Pilate. You proclaimed these allegations to people in the street, stripped off your clothes and threw yourself in the river. You then invaded the Executive Committee of the Writers' Union in your undershorts, repeating your allegations, overturning the supper table, and demanding police action with machine-guns. The question is this: Does a normal person set about apprehending a criminal in this way? If you are normal, as you say you are, you are bound to reply: No. Am I right? *(Confers with NURSE.)* Good. *(To BEZDOMNY.)* Good. So you want to leave?

BEZDOMNY: Yes.

STRAVINSKY: *(To NURSE.)* Please arrange for the patient to be discharged.

BEZDOMNY: Thank you!

STRAVINSKY: But don't put anyone else in this room. Don't change the bedclothes. He'll be back again within two hours.

NURSE: Yes doctor. *(Pause.)*

STRAVINSKY: *(To BEZDOMNY.)* You're not mad. You're quite sane.

BEZDOMNY: He must be stopped!

STRAVINSKY: You need a period of rest: a recharging of the batteries of the mind. Nurse Praskovya Fyodorovna will bring you anything you need – books, papers, pens – write it all down, step by step, exactly as it happened. Then study it. Make sense of it. All right? But don't dwell too much on Pontius Pilate, there's a good fellow! *(He goes, conferring with the NURSE.)*

*Cross-fade to B. PILATE and CAIAPHAS. The High Priest wears a grey robe with black head-dress and insignia.*

PILATE: High Priest, it was kind of you to come so promptly. Suffocating, this heat, exhausting… I have seen the man Ha-Notsri. I have examined him and confirmed your sentence.

CAIAPHAS: We are much obliged.

PILATE: We have four criminals for execution: Dismas, Hestus, Bar-Abba and now Ha-Notsri. In honour of your feast however, we are permitted to exercise clemency.

CAIAPHAS: With respect, we should wish to advise you on this point.

PILATE: And we should not wish to proceed without your advice High Priest.

CAIAPHAS: We are much obliged.

PILATE: It's cruel this heat. Is it always so oppressive?

CAIAPHAS: The month of Nisan has been unusually harsh this year.

PILATE: We may release one prisoner. Of the four, Dismas and Hestus do not qualify. They have incited the people against Caesar and must be punished. They were apprehended by our police. The law cannot bend for them.

CAIAPHAS: Agreed.

PILATE: Good. This leaves Bar-Abba and Ha-Notsri.

CAIAPHAS: The Sanhedrin recommends the release of Bar-Abba.

PILATE: You surprise me.

CAIAPHAS: We have deliberated.

PILATE: So have I, most carefully. This situation is delicate. We cannot afford to release the wrong man.

CAIAPHAS: We recommend Bar-Abba.

PILATE: Let's examine his case.

CAIAPHAS: We have examined both cases.

PILATE: It appears to me that Bar-Abba is immeasurably the more dangerous of the two. He has made direct appeals to rebellion, openly threatening the authority of myself and of you the Sanhedrin. You were wise to apprehend him. We are grateful. It would be foolish to let him go, don't you think?

CAIAPHAS: We recommend his release.

PILATE: What about Ha-Notsri?

CAIAPHAS: He should be killed.

PILATE: But he's mad. He's harmless. He's a dreamer. He was arrested for making absurd speeches which no one in his right mind would take seriously.

CAIAPHAS: We have taken him seriously. *(Pause.)*

PILATE: It's suffocating.

CAIAPHAS: There is a thunderstorm brewing.

PILATE: Stifling…

CAIAPHAS: The matter is concluded then?

PILATE: I am stifled by your presence High Priest.

CAIAPHAS: We are accustomed to the procurator choosing his words with care.

PILATE: You are making a fool of me.

CAIAPHAS: Are we overheard?

PILATE: We have a weak-minded vagrant whose only crime is his own naivety –

CAIAPHAS: Take care Procurator.

PILATE: *You* must take care. You have complained of me to Caesar on more than one occasion, and I have handled the resulting complications with good grace. The time is rapidly approaching however, when I shall have to complain of *you*. I shall have to report that you are using your authority to recommend the release of a convicted terrorist. I shall have to apply for increased security forces and severe restrictions upon your privileges. I do not wish to do this. The Roman presence is pacific by nature, but we are nonetheless responsible for your people's continued safety.

CAIAPHAS: And so you must remove Ha-Notsri. He has urged the overthrow of our institutions. He has cursed our faith. He had defamed our heritage.

PILATE: He is mad!

CAIAPHAS: He will confuse the people, rouse the rabble and provide you with your perfect excuse to send in troops and armaments, to cordon off our nation and wipe us out. Your defence of him has proved to me that his activities are sponsored by Rome, to our detriment.

PILATE: That is ridiculous.

CAIAPHAS: So we recommend most strongly that sentence is carried out.

PILATE: He spoke *against* Caesar. We have evidence. *(Pause.)*

CAIAPHAS: *(Smiles.)* Then you have no choice. *(Pause.)*

PILATE: You arranged this.

CAIAPHAS: Take care.

PILATE: You bribed a man to denounce him.

CAIAPHAS: Walls have ears Procurator.

PILATE: To twist his words into treasonable evidence which would hang him.

CAIAPHAS: I think we have said enough. The crowd is waiting. You have to address them. They wish to know your decision. They wish to get on with the business of erasing the blots in our society. We recommend the release of Bar-Abba. The choice is yours Procurator, but the consequences may be with you for some time, if you choose foolishly.

*Cross-fade to BEZDOMNY on the block in D, a grey towel and wash-basin beside him.*

BEZDOMNY: I feel sick. I can't think. I can't decide. I can't choose. I am sane. Why do I care so much for the Chairman who lost his head? He rejected my work. Why should I crusade for the arrest of his murderer? Where has it got me? The mad-house! As soon as I cease to think of him, I shall be normal. As soon as I get over it, I shall be cured, I shall be released. I have to make up my mind...

*Cross-fade to PILATE on B. He addresses the crowd.*

PILATE: Four criminals, arrested in Jerusalem for murder, incitement to rebellion, contempt of the law and blasphemy, have been condemned to death. Their execution will be carried out today on Mount Golgotha. The names of these felons are: Dismas, Hestus, Bar-Abba and Ha-Notsri. But only three of them are to be executed; for in accordance with law and custom, in honour of the Feast of the Passover, Caesar, in his magnanimity, will, on the advice of the Sanhedrin, render back to one of these convicted men, his miserable life...

*Cross-fade to CAIPHAS and JUDAS OF KARIOTH, dimly on C. JUDAS wears a grey robe.*

JUDAS: High Priest... It's me... Judas of Karioth...

CAIPHAS: Were you followed?

JUDAS: No. You said I should come to you for... payment.

CAIPHAS: What did we agree?

JUDAS: Thirty. *(CAIPHAS pays him.)*

*Cross-fade to PILATE on C.*

PILATE: The name of the man who is about to be released among you, is... Bar-Abba.

*Cut to BEZDOMNY kneeling, washing his face and hands.*

BEZDOMNY: Gone. Washed away. Washed clean...

*THE MASTER enters from A. He wears the grey uniform and a black skull-cap bearing in silver, the letter "M". He is blind.*

MASTER: May I join you?

BEZDOMNY: Who are you? How did you get in? It's locked.

MASTER: *(Rattling a bunch of keys.)* The nurse is a dear soul but terribly absent-minded. She thinks I can't hear where she puts them down. Don't tell her.

BEZDOMNY: Are you running away?

MASTER: Are you?

BEZDOMNY: I'm normal. I'm a writer.

MASTER: Don't.

BEZDOMNY: What?

MASTER: Write any more.

BEZDOMNY: *(Passionate.)* I have to!

MASTER: Are you violent?

BEZDOMNY: I was yesterday.

MASTER: What did you do?

BEZDOMNY: I lost control. I was with the Chairman of the Writers' Union when he was killed. I went mad with grief as if I'd lost my most valued friend. I now realize that it was no loss at all. He was a hindrance. He despised my work. I'm glad he's gone.

MASTER: Will the new Chairman be kinder to you?

BEZDOMNY: I don't know. I don't care, as long as I'm free to write what I think.

MASTER: And being normal, you'll be able to do that?

BEZDOMNY: Oh yes.

MASTER: But normal people *don't* write what they think. The Executive Committee sees to that. If you write what you think, ten to one, you'll be dismissed as *ab*normal.

BEZDOMNY: I write to extol the State.

MASTER: You have to write as the Committee thinks, if you want to be normal.

BEZDOMNY: The Committee will think as *I* think, when they read what I've written.

MASTER: What is it about?

BEZDOMNY: The indestructibility of the State. A man tempted me yesterday to permit loop-holes. The idea unhinged me for a while. I'm glad to say I've rejected it. The state of my theme is as strong as ever.

MASTER: Nothing can leak out?

BEZDOMNY: Nothing!

MASTER: How is it contained?

BEZDOMNY: By law.

MASTER: What happens to those who think their own thoughts and question the law?

BEZDOMNY: They are removed.

MASTER: How are they caught? By stealth?

BEZDOMNY: It doesn't matter how they're caught.

MASTER: Corruption? Informers?

BEZDOMNY: They *have* to be caught! That's all that matters. If a man thinks for himself and his thoughts lead to actions which subvert the collective strength of the State, he has to be caught!

MASTER: But if the means of catching is corrupt –

BEZDOMNY: He has to be removed!

MASTER: Corruption rots. Suppression stultifies.

BEZDOMNY: *(Realizing.)* You're blind. *(Pause.)* Why are you here?

MASTER: I used to write. I'm a voluntary patient.

BEZDOMNY: What is your name?

MASTER: I've given it up.

BEZDOMNY: What was your name?

MASTER: I've forgotten.

BEZDOMNY: What do they call you?

MASTER: The one person who mattered called me the Master.

BEZDOMNY: Who was he?

MASTER: Who was *she*?

*Pause. Quiet music begins.*

When I first saw her, she was carrying some yellow flowers. I wasn't blind then. She was beautiful, and so sad. There was a deep loneliness in her eyes.

*Light discovers MARGARITA on B. She wears a long grey dress and carries a bunch of dying yellow flowers. She lets them fall, turns away. The MASTER approaches her, picks up the flowers.*

Your flowers... They're dying...

*She moves away.*

*(Aside.)* She walked away. I exchanged the flowers for some red roses. *(Does so.)* I ran after her. I had to speak to her. I couldn't let her go. She was waiting by the bridge.

*MARGARITA is on the steps between B and C. The MASTER goes to her.*

I'm sorry. I thought you might prefer roses. I believe red to be a stronger colour. Yellow is no good to anyone: the colour of cowardice. Will you take them?

## LOVE LEAPS OUT

MARGARITA: *(Sings.)* What can I do?
Should I run?
Common sense –
I have none.
I am caught –
can't get away
like a victim
at bay. *(She turns.)*

BOTH: Love leaps out like a murderer!
Shock of a switch-blade knife!
Gleams and blinds and jolts me
like lightning – to life!

| MARGARITA: | | MASTER: | |
|---|---|---|---|
| | The wound | | I am alive. |
| | is deep | | I was dead. |
| | as love | | Now my heart |
| | runs red; | | is in my head! |
| | fear | | I am insane, |

| | |
|---|---|
| bleeds away | I was wise. |
| Now shame | Now the flame |
| is dead; | is in my eyes! |
| the reason | I was sick, |
| screams | now I'm whole. |
| as the mind | She quickens |
| is torn; | my soul! |
| and dreams | No state |
| flood the brain | is as it was |
| as the soul | of a sudden |
| is born! | because – |

BOTH: Love leaps out like a murderer!
Shock of a switch-blade knife!
Gleams and blinds and jolts me
like lightning – to life!

*He gives her the roses. They kiss. He turns away, sits on the steps to D. MARGARITA lies on the table on C.*

MASTER: She came to my basement flat every day at noon. I began waiting for her as soon as the sun rose. After ten minutes, I would sit at my window and start listening for the creak of the gate. I would wait all morning, every day, my heart in my mouth, listening for that creak, the crunch of her foot-step, the rustle of her skirt as she came down the steps…

## EVERY DAY

MARGARITA: Every day we vow to love each other.
Every day we skim the cream.
Suddenly we disagree and rock the bed.
We rage and roar and scream.
We vow forever to hate each other.
We tear, we weep, we claw.
We cling a little closer as we wrestle and then
we feast to the full once more!
We sail the seas, rough-ride the waves.
We sigh, we clamour, we sing,

and we lie in final silence only
breathing… breathing… breathing…

MASTER: I started on my book. It flooded out of me. It was
born of our passion! It cast a spell over her. She read it
and re-read it. She learnt to type and sang the words aloud
as they clack-clacked onto the page. She called me the
Master. I called her Margarita. I never knew her real name.
She never knew mine. I finished my book. I offered it to a
publisher.

*Light on PUBLISHER on B.*

PUBLISHER: It's good – uncommonly good. It's your first isn't
it? Remarkable. Do you mind if I hang on to it.

MASTER: He kept it for a fortnight.

PUBLISHER: I'm sorry, it's just not suitable. In any case, we
have enough material from established authors to keep us
busy for at least a couple of years. We'll let you know if
we feel we could, at a later date, consider anything further
from you.

*His light fades.*

MASTER: I was disappointed of course. I suffered for several
days the agony of the rejected writer. Then one day, I
opened my newspaper, and there it was – a full-page
article!

*Light on four CRITICS on B.*

1 CRITIC: The enemy strikes!

2 CRITIC: Obscenity!

3 CRITIC: Depravity!

4 CRITIC: Rotten to the core!

MASTER: My work reviewed as if I were a published writer!

1 CRITIC: Vile perversions of a diseased mind!

2 CRITIC: He drags his gutter meanderings into print!

3 CRITIC: Exhibits the rancid underbelly of the individualist
carcase!

4 CRITIC: Long since buried by the will of the State!

MASTER: Then a day or two later, another article, in another paper.

1 CRITIC: Shun this filth!

2 CRITIC: Stamp out this cancer!

3 CRITIC: Purge the State of these foul imaginings!

4 CRITIC: Cleanse the people of this blight!

*Their light fades.*

MASTER: Again and again, more and more, hammering, desecrating, wrenching me to pieces! I became ill. My eyes began to fail. I couldn't eat. I couldn't sleep. I was bitterly depressed. That was the first stage. Then came amazement. In literally every line of those articles, you could detect a sense of unease, a falseness, in spite of their confident, rigorous language. I couldn't help feeling that the critics weren't saying what they *wanted* to say. They were ranting and raving from their own frustration. They couldn't pour out their own personal furies, so they hacked at me instead! Then came the third stage. Fear – not of the articles: something much worse, much deeper...

MARGARITA: We must get you out of here, far away. Leave all this behind. I can arrange it.

MASTER: I felt the black autumn would burst through my window and flood the room like a torrent of thick ink! I screamed, I cringed, I wanted to run, I couldn't get out. I grabbed my manuscript. I lit the stove. I bundled it in, page after page: the months of labour, the weeks of devotion, the hours of tumbling inspiration, all burning, dying –

MARGARITA: *(Amazed.)* Why? Why?

MASTER: I hate it!

MARGARITA: It's your life!

MASTER: It terrifies me.

MARGARITA: You're going to write it again, every word! I shall take you away and sit over you until you have rewritten every word!

MASTER: She promised that when she came to see me the next day, it would be forever. She would never leave me.

MARGARITA: We'll go far away from here.

MASTER: We'd live in peace where no one could reach us.

MARGARITA: Tomorrow when I come, we'll go far away, far away… *(She goes.)*

MASTER: *(To BEZDOMNY.)* She didn't come the next day, nor the next.

BEZDOMNY: Where was she?

MASTER: I don't know.

BEZDOMNY: Where did she go each night?

MASTER: She never told me. *(Pause.)* On the third day when she didn't come, I knew it was over. I was ill, I was nearly blind. I was going mad. I knew of this clinic. As long as I could see, I could make my way here. I was admitted as a voluntary patient. I've been here for six months. I feel secure. I'm no longer afraid of the dark. Decisions are taken for me. I no longer have to think for myself.

BEZDOMNY: You must! What about your book? You must work on it!

MASTER: I can't see.

BEZDOMNY: I could help you. We could work together. What was it about, your book? Tell me. What was the subject?

MASTER: The Devil.

BEZDOMNY: What does he do? If you tell me, I could write it down. We needn't tell anyone. I've plenty of paper.

MASTER: He comes to Moscow, disguised as a professor of Black Magic.

BEZDOMNY: Why?

MASTER: To remind man that he is mortal.

BEZDOMNY: How does he do that?

MASTER: *(Smiles.)* He prophesies of sudden death. He exposes corruption within the committee system. And he stages,

with his retinue, a Black Magic Sensation at the Variety
Theatre…

*Fanfare music. Cut to GEORGE BENGALSKY, The Master of
Ceremonies in a follow-spot on C. He wears black tails, grey shirt
and tie.*

BENGALSKY: Ladies and gentlemen! The Variety Theatre
is honoured to present – I don't believe it! I must be
mistaken! Our audience has doubled in size since the
intermission! Half Moscow seems to be here tonight.
Which reminds me. I met a friend of mine the other day
and I said to him: Why didn't you come to our show?
Half the town was their last night! And he said: I live in
the other half! *(babum!)* Well, as I was saying, the Variety
Theatre is honoured to present for your delight and for
your edification, that fabulously famous artiste from
abroad – Monsieur Woland! The Manipulator of Miracles
and Magnificent Maestro of Black Magic! – which as we
all know, is a sly superstition and a craft of cunning – for
Maestro Woland is a Pastmaster Trickster, a Conjuror of
Carefully Concocted Caprice! Watch his act, ladies and
gentlemen! See the join and spot the trick! For Monsieur
Woland himself has graciously agreed to conclude his act
with a step-by-step scientific revelation of his very own
breath-taking technique! All will be divulged! No mystery
will be spared! Illusion will be shattered, and superstition
laid bare before you! So it only remains, ladies and
gentlemen, since none of us can bear the suspense one
moment longer, for your own Variety Theatre, to present
for you tonight: Monsieur the Maestro Woland!!

*Cut to STAGE MANAGER and DEPUTY in the control box.*

DEPUTY: Who is Monsieur Woland? Where's he from?

SM: No one knows. But have you heard where he's staying?

DEPUTY: Where?

SM: In the apartment of the Chairman of the Writers' Union!

DEPUTY: The one who was killed? I don't believe it!

SM: Number 50, 302A Sadovaya Street. The Chairman
of the Tenants' Association arrived to sort through the

deceased's effects and he found Monsieur Woland already
in occupation!

DEPUTY: That's not possible!

SM: With his woman, his boy and his cat!

DEPUTY: Apartments have to be allocated. There's a waiting
list.

SM: Nothing could be done.

*Cut to C. Fanfare music. WOLAND in black top hat, tails and
cloak with red lining, accompanied by HELLA, AZAZELLO and
BEHEMOTH. Music hall song and dance.*

## TRUCKS AND TRAINS AND TRAMS

WOLAND: How are things in Moscow?
Has it changed at all?
Are the people colourful?
Are they having a ball?

AZAZELLO: As far as we can see sir
the city outwardly –

HELLA: is running smoothly on its rails –

BEHEMOTH: as grey as grey can be!

ALL: They've got the
telephone radio cars and cabs
and trucks and trains and trams
and police patrols to combat crime
and regulate traffic jams;
and a city committee that sits so pretty
with folio file and form
to denounce and deal with those who dare
to deviate from the norm!

WOLAND: But what of individuals?
What do they think about?
The intellectual avant-garde?

RETINUE: They don't allow them out!

WOLAND: But why in Heaven's name is this?

It surely can't be so!
What've they got to nourish the mind?
I'd really like to know.

RETINUE: They've got the
 telephone radio cars and cabs
 and trucks and trains and trams
 and police patrols to combat crime
 and regulate traffic jams,
 and a city committee that sits so pretty
 with folio file and form
 to denounce and deal with those who dare
 to deviate from the norm!

WOLAND: But comrades mine, I am concerned
 and saddened I am too,
 to feel there is this rigid crust
 that can't be broken through.
 For surely someone somewhere lives
 whose inspiration soars
 sufficiently to lift the load

AZAZELLO: No sir –

WOLAND: How so – ?

HELLA: Because…

WOLAND: Don't tell me!

BEHEMOTH: They've got the –

WOLAND: Let's have it!

*They display a song-sheet.*

ALL: Telephone radio cars and cabs
 and trucks and trains and trams
 and police patrols to combat crime
 and regulate traffic jams,
 and a city committee that sits so pretty
 with folio file and form
 to denounce and deal with those who dare
 to deviate from the norm!

WOLAND: One more time, what have they got?

ALL: *(Rousing the audience to clap and sing.)*
    They've got the
    telephone radio cars and cabs
    and trucks and trains and trams
    and police patrols to combat crime
    and regulate traffic jams,
    and a city committee that sits so pretty
    with folio file and form
    to denounce and deal with those who
    dare to deviate from the norm!

*Cut to control box.*

DEPUTY: It's scandalous! How were they allowed – ?

SM: Haven't you heard? They turned up in the Treasurer's office at the Variety Theatre and insisted that the manager had booked them.

DEPUTY: The cheek!

SM: There was a note of authorization.

DEPUTY: A forgery.

SM: It was down in black and white and there were posters to prove it.

DEPUTY: Incredible! Preposterous!

*Cut to C. BENGALSKY enters applauding the actors who bow.*

BENGALSKY: Unbelievable! Fantastic! Amazing! It is clear, ladies and gentlemen, from that rollicking rip-roaring refrain, that our guest artiste from abroad is delighted with Moscow's technological progress!

WOLAND: Did I say I was delighted?

BEHEMOTH: You said no such thing.

WOLAND: Then what is he talking about?

HELLA: He's lying.

BENGALSKY: *(Grinning.)* It's how it came over to me. It's how it came over to the audience!

217

AZAZELLO: D'you hear, you're a liar.

BENGALSKY: Now let's not get personal –

WOLAND: *(Cold.)* This man, ladies and gentlemen, is a liar. *(Pause.)*

BENGALSKY: Well isn't that amazing? But seriously, joking apart –

BEHEMOTH: *(Pushing him.)* Get off!

BENGALSKY: *(Stumbling.)* On with the show!

AZAZELLO: *(Displaying pack of cards.)* Here's a quick slick trick…

*Cut to control box.*

SM: I've never seen anything like it.

DEPUTY: The M.C. is a man of proven integrity.

SM: What are they doing now?

DEPUTY: They're throwing a pack of cards at each other.

SM: Pitiful.

DEPUTY: The cat! It's swallowed the cards! The whole pack!

*Cut to C.*

BEHEMOTH: *(Burps.)*

MAN IN AUDIENCE: It's a trick!

AZAZELLO: The gentleman at the back says it's a trick.

HELLA: House lights!  *(House lights.)*

MAN IN AUDIENCE: How is it done?

WOLAND: Look in your pocket sir. That pack of cards is to be found in your wallet between a three-rouble note and a summons to appear in court for non-payment of alimony to your ex-wife!

MAN IN AUDIENCE: *(Devastated.)* My God!

WOLAND: Keep it as a souvenir sir!

MAN IN AUDIENCE: I'm ruined! I'm disgraced…! *(Leaves in confusion.)*

WOMAN IN AUDIENCE: He's a plant! It's obvious –

AZAZELLO: If that is so madam, then so are you!

HELLA: Look in your bag!

WOLAND: ...where you will find yet another pack of cards, enclosed in a wad of crisp and crinkly bank-notes, totalling – wait for it – one thousand roubles!

WOMAN IN AUDIENCE: It's true! I'm rich! A thousand roubles!

PEOPLE IN AUDIENCE: Play that trick on me!

– And me!

– Me too...

AZAZELLO: All right sir!

HELLA: You've said it!

BEHEMOTH: *(Raising his Browning automatic.)* Stand by to panic! *(Bang!.)*

*Cut to control box.*

SM: What is going on?

DEPUTY: Pandemonium!

SM: There's a cascade of bank notes!

DEPUTY: Thousands of them!

SM: Tumbling down from the ceiling!

DEPUTY: They're scrambling for them! It's chaos!

SM: People will be crushed!

DEPUTY: It's irrational! It's not happening!

*Cut to C. BENGALSKY returns.*

BENGALSKY: All right ladies and gentlemen, relax, let's relax. Let's see some of that cast-iron control that we're famous for! Come on gentlemen, ladies, comrades all! The collective will! Cleave to the girders of the Tower of State! Firmly and bravely! Let's have control... Thank you, thank you ladies and gentlemen, thank you...

WOLAND: *(Stepping forward.)* Thank you.

*The audience is calmed. The DEMONS begin to molest BENGALSKY. He tries to make light of it.*

BENGALSKY: We have just had the privilege – and a remarkable privilege it is too! – of seeing at first hand the effects of what has come to be known as mass hypnosis! A pure and simple scientific exercise ladies and gentlemen, clearly demonstrating that there is nothing, absolutely nothing supernatural about magic. So let's now ask the Maestro to show us exactly how he carried out this experiment. Attend ladies and gentlemen! The cogs and spring of the magic machine are about to be disconnected for your own collective examination! For you will see ladies and gentlemen, those so-called bank-notes evaporate as suddenly and as logically as they appeared –

AUDIENCE: Boo! Shame! They're real! They're mine! Shame! Boo…!

BENGALSKY: I give you my word! I stake my life on it!

*BEHEMOTH leaps on him thrashing and tearing.*

AUDIENCE: Kill him! Throttle him! Wrench his head off!

*Cut to control box.*

DEPUTY: Monstrous!

SM: What's he *doing*?

DEPUTY: He's tearing at him!

SM: He's wrenching off his *head*!

DEPUTY: Revolting! Sickening!

SM: Look at the blood!

DEPUTY: I can't! I can't!

SM: Fountains of it are shooting up and drenching the audience!

DEPUTY: He's not dead!

*Cut to C. WOLAND stands astride BENGALSKY's HEAD which rests on the table.*

WOLAND: Any more requests?

HEAD: Call a doctor.

WOLAND: Do you believe in magic?

HEAD: No mystery is insoluble.

WOLAND: Do you believe in God?

HEAD: Call a doctor. I'm bleeding.

WOLAND: Do you believe in the Devil?

HEAD: God and the Devil do not exist.

AUDIENCE: – Let him go…

    – You're torturing him…

WOLAND: Do you believe in the Power of Good?

HEAD: I believe that man is the master of all things.

WOLAND: How do you explain what has just happened?

HEAD: It's an optical illusion. Call a doctor!

WOLAND: Why, if it's not happening?

HEAD: I'm dying! Help me! I'm bleeding to death!

WOLAND: Shall we forgive him ladies and gentlemen?

HEAD: Reassemble me please!

AUDIENCE: – Let him go!

    – Stop tormenting him!

    – Put him back!

HEAD: I'm sorry…Please, let me go…I believe in the fears and
horrors of this moment. Isn't that enough?

WOLAND: Do you believe in compassion?

HEAD: Yes.

WOLAND: When it suits you.

HEAD: Yes!

WOLAND: Do you believe in the freedom of the individual to
think for himself?

HEAD: Help me…

WOLAND: Ladies and gentlemen, the salvation of this man
rests with you.

AZAZELLO: Who believes in magic?

HELLA: Can we have a show of hands please?

WOLAND: Individual beliefs only.

AZAZELLO: No collective impressions.

HELLA: Think inwardly.

WOLAND: Think for yourselves.

HEAD: Save me…Please put me back…

*Cut to control box.*

DEPUTY: It's sabotage.

SM: It's blackmail.

DEPUTY: He's undermining the Tower of State.

SM: He's wrecking our collective strength.

DEPUTY: *(Appalled.)* They're voting for belief in magic!

SM: It's mass hypnosis. They'll wake up with a bump.

DEPUTY: He's put the head back on.

SM: The M.C. is a broken man.

DEPUTY: It'll affect him for life…

*Cross-fade to C. BENGALSKY dimly stumbling away.*

BENGALSKY: Where's my head…? Give me back my head…
I want my head back please… Have you seen my head…?
My head…

*Music swells as WOLAND appears on C. A mirror-ball showers the theatre with stars. AZAZELLO, BEHEMOTH and HELLA appear with yards of imaginary gowns and rails of invisible suits.*

## LISTEN LADIES

WOLAND: Listen ladies, see before you,
for we proudly announce:
We have dresses, silk and satin,
fur stoles, velvet gowns.

And my lords, we have brought you
handsome hats, sleek shoes,
shirts aplenty, all sizes,
fine suits for you to choose…

*One by one the PEOPLE IN THE AUDIENCE are drawn on to the stage. They remove their grey clothes and try on and parade in the fantastic "costumes", assisted by WOLAND and the DEVILS.*

…Try it lady, feel the texture.
Step up sir, no charge.
We will gladly ma'am replace it
should the girth prove too large.

Over here, be so good sir
to disrobe, if you please.
Leave the grey clothes behind you
wear the silk sir, with ease.

Jewelled slipper, patent leather,
parfum de Paree.
No charge, none at all sir.
Every fitting is free…

*The PEOPLE are dancing and whirling, entranced by the costumes.*

Wear the gown, spangled diamonds,
dance gaily 'cross the floor,
choose gladly, step out proudly.
There's more, and more!

Love the beauty, feel the magic,
each lady, every lord,
fulfilled, so full of pleasure,
admired and adored…

*Gradually the stars go out and the air chills as they realize they are in their underclothes. The RETINUE disperses.*

Through the evening, till the morning,
till a chill nips the air,
till you slowly grow to realize
that the garments are not there.

All you're wearing is your body,
just skin, flesh and bone.
You're frightened and you shiver,
just you, all alone…

*They are still.*

How fragile is magic.
How thin is the air.
How cold is the truth
when no clothes are there…

*He goes. The unclothed PEOPLE shuffle to the block on D and crowd on to it. The MASTER is lit down left on D.*

MASTER: They flood into the street in their fine robes. The wind gathers and whips the clothes from their backs. The police move in and herd them in hundreds into the psychiatric wards. There's not enough staff to cope. The system is crumbling…

*He joins the crowded mass on the block and is lost among them. MARGARITA sings from A.*

## I FLEW

MARGARITA: I flew in the wind.
I flew as he fell.
I flew like a whisper.
I left him in hell.

My love was removed.
I flew to the sun.
My love lay blind.
His day was done.

The cowards we were!
I saw where we sinned.
But I couldn't descend
in the wind…

*The CROWD on the block raise their hands to her as her light fades. Silence. Fade to black.*

*End of Act One.*

# ACT TWO

*MARGARITA and BORIS MIKHAILOVICH, her husband, sit at table on B at supper. BORIS eats hungrily and reads a newspaper. MARGARITA does not eat.*

BORIS: They buried him today, Chairman of the Writers'
Union. Sorry business. They lost his head. It'd been
severed by the tram wheels. The undertakers took great
pains to stick it back on for the lying-in-state, and some
thief ran off with it. Not eating my dear?

MARGARITA: *(Aside.)* This is my husband, Boris Mikhailovich:
strong, handsome, kind-hearted, honest. His work is of
national importance. He's an architect.

BORIS: Ugly forces at work. Look at that fiasco at the
Variety Theatre. The audience came flooding out in their
underclothes! Invaded the bar and tried to buy drinks with
buttons and toffee papers! Seems they were seduced into it
by mass hypnosis and black magic...

MARGARITA: He doesn't know of my love for the Master. I
couldn't tell him. It would break his heart.

BORIS: We're at the crossroads, crisis time. They say it's
inevitable, after a dozen years of enlightenment, for the
wreckers to move in. They're not content, you see. They
forget. The beast of state has a million legs that have to
be trained to keep in step. Else they trip up and we all go
tumbling into the psychiatric clinic.

MARGARITA: Every day at noon, I used to visit the Master. I
lived for those brief moments of passion and hope. My life
at home was a shadow without him.

BORIS: I made a vow today my dear. I was looking at our
plans for the Tower of State: the perfect construction,
unassailable, an example to waverers of what we have
achieved! It has three geometrical chambers, one
above another, perpetually moving, at different speeds:
cubiform for legislation, pyramidal for administration
and cylindrical for propaganda. And if I get my way with

the committee my dear, there'll be one further chamber, of elastic proportions, out of sight being subterraneous, for the rehabilitation of dissidents. It's good isn't it? And here's the point: I vowed today to dedicate my work in its construction, to you.

MARGARITA: Three days ago, I decided to leave my husband.

BORIS: We've been married for ten years. I'd like to think that our marriage is as strong against all weathers as the Tower itself!

MARGARITA: I told the Master I would return to him the next day, to stay with him for ever.

BORIS: What do you think of it? Let's have some enthusiasm. Come on!

MARGARITA: But I couldn't do it. I delayed. I was sick with terror.

BORIS: What is it? *(Astounded.)* Oh my dear... What a bullet-head I am! I spout and rant and gorge myself, and you sit there with the patience of Mother Russia! You need rest, and you shall have it. I shall watch over you, and your precious burden, every moment. I shall not let you out of my sight!

MARGARITA: Three days have passed...

BORIS: Our child shall be a symbol like the Tower of State of the indestructibility... *(Sleeps.)*

MARGARITA: I slipped out at noon. I came to the basement flat. He wasn't there. He'd gone. The flat was empty. It was over.

*Fade to black. Light discovers YESHUA crucified naked, high up on the scaffolding above A. MURIBELLUM sits on the steps beneath him, playing knuckle-bones. Far below, on the D block, sits MATTHEW in a grey tunic. He has a water-flask, wax tablet and stilus, and a bread-knife in his belt. PILATE stands near him, disguised in a grey cloak and cowl.*

MATTHEW: Do you know him? The one in the middle. I do. Yeshua Ha-Notsri. He's my closest friend. It's all my fault he's up there. Look at the flies! He shakes his head and they're straight back, sucking at him! I am worse than those flies! *(Pause.)* I used to be a tax collector. I listened to him. I argued with him. He said all men are good. I believed in him. I threw my money in the road and followed him. I wrote down everything he said.

YESHUA: *(Groans.)*

MATTHEW: What did he say?

YESHUA: God help me…

MATTHEW: *(Writing.)* My God, my God, why hast thou forsaken me!

PILATE: Those were not his words.

MATTHEW: He fulfils the prophets. He is the Lamb of God that taketh away the sins of the world. Take away *my* sins Lord! Take away my *sins! (To PILATE.)* I let him go! For one moment, I let him out of my sight. We were staying in Bethphagy with a gardener. We were going to walk to Jerusalem in the cool of the evening. But Yeshua said he had something urgent to do there. He set off when I wasn't looking! Why won't he *die*? God let him die! Please God! You are deaf! You are evil! I curse you God! I spit at you!

*Rumble of thunder.*

PILATE: It's going to rain. It'll drive off the flies.

YESHUA: Water…

MURIBELLUM: You what?

YESHUA: I need water…

MURIBELLUM: It's not allowed, and you know that. So there's no point in asking, all right?

MATTHEW: I was going to kill him. When he was in the cart going up the hill. I was going to leap onto the cart and kill him and then kill myself. "Yeshua, I am your friend, your slave and your friend! I shall save you and save myself with you! I shall spare you from this evil world!" But I had no knife.

PILATE: *(Indicating knife.)* What's that?

MATTHEW: I stole it. I was running for the city gate. There was a baker's shop. I went in. I asked for a loaf. When his back was turned, I took the knife. I ran out and out of the gate. I was brave! I was going to do it! But it was too late. They were nearly there. The soldiers had cordoned off the area... *(Pause.)* It's so hot... *(Drinks from his flask, then throws it to the ground and stamps on it.)* I am a fool! I am a worm! And my father is a worm! And my mother is a worm!

YESHUA: Water!

MATTHEW: He said water! Quick! *(Retrieves his flask – it is empty.)*

Oh God – *God!*

*Pause.*

MURIBELLUM: *(To YESHUA.)* You're lucky. Did you know that? You fainted for an hour. Nodded off like a baby...

MATTHEW: Perform a miracle God. It's been nearly three hours. Make him die please God!

MURIBELLUM: Beats me what you're doing up there. You didn't kill anyone. You didn't rape anyone. All you did was shoot your mouth off about the world being good. It's my opinion, you being up there has proved you wrong. Eh? Eh? What do you say to that?

MATTHEW: *(Praying.)* That man is good. He is the one good man and you permit him to suffer like this. You have failed me God. I no longer accept you.

MURIBELLUM: You've got horse-flies all over your groin. We're not permitted to knock them off. If we did it for you, we'd have to do it for the others. Then where would we be?

YESHUA: It's no one's fault. I blame no one. *(Expires.)*

PILATE: He's dead.

MATTHEW: *(Writing.)* And the veil of the Temple was rent from top to bottom. There was an earthquake. The rocks split and the graves opened. And the centurion who was with him was sore afraid and he said: "Truly this is a good man!"

MURIBELLUM: You've lost me twenty drachmas, you know that? We had a wager, the lads and me. They said you wouldn't last out three hours.

PILATE: Will you burn your writings?

MURIBELLUM: *(Going.)* Funny thing death. Can't grasp it. Seen it so many times, but I couldn't tell you what happens...

PILATE: They'll be misinterpreted. Better to burn them and forget all about it.

*Thunder, lightning. Storm breaks.*

MATTHEW: *YESHUA...!!*

*In violent lightning and thunderclaps, to the music of "O Sacred Head..." from the St Matthew Passion played on the organ, MATTHEW runs up to the cross, climbs the scaffolding, hacks at the ropes with his bread-knife. YESHUA's body tumbles down on him. He carries it away. The storm subsides.*

PILATE: Forget all about it. Rub out the evidence. Delete the facts. Must work, day and night. Never have the leisure to think. Never let the mind play tricks.

*Cross-fade to MARGARITA lying on B. Beside her is BORIS, asleep.*

## AS I LAY

MARGARITA: *(Sings.)*
As I lay with my husband I dreamed,
as he rode and I lay, it seemed
I waited alone in a desolate place.
He rode and rode as I dreamed.

The sky was leaden with grey
sagging clouds and rooks that cried:
a swollen stream, a crippled bridge,
joyless trees either side.

And in my dream I saw
with aching eyes dried raw,
a distant shack by an aspen tree,
a closed door I saw.

I moved through the lifeless air,
and tore my feet on tufts of thorn:
not a breath of wind, not a hope of life.
To the shack my body was drawn.

And it opened, flung wide!
A man was standing inside!
The Master living, reaching for me!
My own, my love! I cried.

I ran for miles to the man.
He moved his lips, he spoke;
but the dream words I heard not,
for I awoke...

*AZAZELLO had appeared beside her.*

AZAZELLO: Stay asleep.

MARGARITA: Who are you?

AZAZELLO: Forgive me but you must be Margarita.

MARGARITA: How do you know my secret name?

AZAZELLO: I bring you an invitation from an eminent foreign
  gentleman.

MARGARITA: Who?

AZAZELLO: Please be calm.

MARGARITA: I'm not interested.

AZAZELLO: I couldn't take a sudden reaction. It's been a
  rough day.

MARGARITA: You're blackmailing me. You know my secret –

AZAZELLO: God's farts woman! I'm helping you! I've sweated
  blood to dredge you out of this tip!

MARGARITA: I'm sorry. I'm so confused.

AZAZELLO: Some thanks I get.

MARGARITA: It's my husband, I don't love him. I love
  someone else, and he's gone.

AZAZELLO: I am Azazello. Does the name toll a knell?

MARGARITA: *(Surprised.)* He wrote about you in his book!

AZAZELLO: We've arrived, just the four of us.

MARGARITA: But he destroyed it. You don't exist.

AZAZELLO: Manuscripts don't burn. *(Pause.)*

MARGARITA: What do you want from me?

AZAZELLO: The Prince of Perdition wants you for his hostess at the Ball.

MARGARITA: No!

AZAZELLO: Hell's heat!

MARGARITA: I couldn't go with another man.

AZAZELLO: You are not invited to "go" with him.

MARGARITA: What does he want then?

AZAZELLO: What do *you* want? Think woman.

MARGARITA: The Master.

AZAZELLO: He is yours. Be hostess as the Ball and you shall have him. Are you coming then?

*They start to go. Sinister music begins.*

MARGARITA: It's not for myself I do this.

AZAZELLO: Oh yes it is.

MARGARITA: It's for the Master.

AZAZELLO: It's for you.

MARGARITA: It is not.

AZAZELLO: Come on, be selfish for once in your life.

MARGARITA: I love him! I want him back!

AZAZELLO: That's better…

MARGARITA: For his sake…

AZAZELLO: And yours… *(They have gone.)*

*By candle-light WOLAND is discovered playing chess with BEHEMOTH on C. He wears a long black night-shirt edged with red, and a black skull-cap, bearing in silver, the letter "W". HELLA stands astride the game. They move the pieces through her legs.*

ALL: And the band plays on for always
  in pools of waning light,
  through a million dreary hallways,
  through starless endless night.

HELLA: The time is approaching. Full is the moon.
  The band is playing a gloomy tune.
  The guests are waiting, in hopelessness,
  for Satan and his hostess.

WOLAND: Check.

BEHEMOTH: Unh?

HELLA: Once each year, I shift my base.
  I smile so wide, it tears my face.
  I leer and loll, I idle and croon,
  for the Ball of the Spring Full Moon.

WOLAND: Moving into check.

BEHEMOTH: Piss.

HELLA: Satan requires a Queen Hostess
  to dampen, flatten, chill, depress.
  So I simper and sag, I linger and lag,
  I niggle and nag,
  I dangle and drag…

BEHEMOTH: Turn her off someone!

HELLA: What queen could be
  half as depressing
  as me!

  *She crawls over WOLAND's body. Music continues.*

WOLAND: Get off me hell-bitch!

HELLA: Oh I like it! I like it!

BEHEMOTH: Want me to lean on her boss?

HELLA: What should I wear to crush the enlightened, to dance
  on their souls?

WOLAND: There are no enlightened souls!

BEHEMOTH: She doesn't understand boss.

WOLAND: Check.

BEHEMOTH: Oh balls.

WOLAND: We have to dig them out you bent and buckled hag.

HELLA: Abuse me! Curse me! *(Climbs all over him.)*

WOLAND: All we have done so far is confuse the dim and confound the dumb and clog the psychiatric clinics with artless drabs.

HELLA: We were wildly successful at the Variety Theatre!

WOLAND: There is no satisfaction in that! Check.

HELLA: None at all my lord. It was wickedly depressing!

BEHEMOTH: Aha! *(Makes a good move.)*

WOLAND: There is one aspect of the ball which you have consistently failed to comprehend, you bag of offal.

HELLA: I adore you for that!

BEHEMOTH: She's as thick as two short planks boss.

WOLAND: We who depress, must not in ourselves be depressed –

HELLA: Beat me…

WOLAND: And those to be depressed should not be *pre*-depressed, you stagnant carcase –

HELLA: Thrash me! Lash me!

WOLAND: They should be joyful, free-thinking, hopeful souls!

HELLA: Rack me with guilt!

WOLAND: So the figure we are urgently seeking at this moment – check –

BEHEMOTH: Unh?

WOLAND: … is the Master of Enlightenment, at present lost, blind and desolate, beneath the heaps of the fallen.

BEHEMOTH: Er, just a minute…

WOLAND: We must resurrect the Master and let his light shine!

HELLA: You mean reverse the process?

BEHEMOTH: *(To chess board.)* I don't quite comprehend…

WOLAND: … that other lights may be kindled and that we, the Dealers in Damnation, may have the ultimate joy of snuffing them out! *(To BEHEMOTH.)* It's check-mate.

HELLA: How do we find this Master my lord?

WOLAND: We encourage our hostess to excavate him.

HELLA: Where do I start?

*AZAZELLO appears with MARGARITA.*

AZAZELLO: I have the honour to present your Queen sir.

HELLA: Aaaaaaaargh!! *(Music stops.)*

BEHEMOTH: *(To HELLA.)* Back you reeking she-slug!

WOLAND: Greetings ma'am.

AZAZELLO: She's asleep.

MARGARITA: Where am I?

WOLAND: Apartment 50, 203A Sadovaya Street.

BEHEMOTH: The body of a friend of a friend of a friend of yours used to live here.

HELLA: I have his head! *(Opens a black hat-box and, cackling, exhibits the head of BERLIOZ.)*

MARGARITA: You stole it!

HELLA: I wanted to pick his brains. *(Flips open the skull and dabbles in the brains.)*

WOLAND: Down crone, or she will wake.

BEHEMOTH: Miaaaaaaow!

*He flies at HELLA. They fight over the head. BEHEMOTH gets it.*

MARGARITA: That head was stolen.

WOLAND: Let them play.

AZAZELLO: We have to work fast sir. The moon is full. We have no time to lose.

WOLAND: Does she know what to do?

AZAZELLO: She lacks courage.

WOLAND: Fetch the cream.

AZAZELLO: Yessir. *(Goes.)*

MARGARITA: What must I do?

WOLAND: Summon the guests.

HELLA: She will fail.

WOLAND: Prove yourself mistress of the Seven Deadly Sins.

HELLA: She is weak.

MARGARITA: What are they?

HELLA: She has no guts.

WOLAND: Behemoth.

BEHEMOTH: Boss? *(Looks up from the head. Strands of brain drool from his mouth.)*

WOLAND: Put it down.

BEHEMOTH: Yes boss.

HELLA: She is afraid. She is a dreamer. She has a conscience. She will break.

WOLAND: Explain the Seven Deadly Sins.

BEHEMOTH: Well there's Pride, Envy, Sloth, Lust –

WOLAND: Not those! The new ones, that stultify man and stagnate life!

AZAZELLO: *(Reappearing with jar of cream.)* Complacency, Bureaucracy, Security, Censorship, Sedation, Corruption and Cowardice.

WOLAND: Thank you.

AZAZELLO: Your cream sir.

HELLA: *(Leaps for it.)* It's mine!

BEHEMOTH: *(Attacking.)* Miaaaaaow!

HELLA: I am the hostess!

WOLAND: Wrench off her leg!

HELLA: No, please no my lord!

BEHEMOTH: Which one boss?

HELLA: I have to dance tonight. Forgive me. Let me serve you.

WOLAND: Honour the Queen.

HELLA: *(Falls before MARGARITA.)* My Queen I honour you. I will never seek to displace you – may you rot in hell!

WOLAND: Homage!

HELLA: … reign in radiance over the Ball tonight, and may your dream be gloriously fulfilled.

WOLAND: Away.

*HELLA, BEHEMOTH and AZAZELLO clear the chess and head.*

*(To MARGARITA.)* Take the cream. Anoint your body. Receive the powers of sorcery. Sail through the night and break the bonds that pinion your Master, gathering guests as each fetter is broken. The Tower of Man will disintegrate before you as you prove yourself Mistress of the Sins. The Ball commences at midnight. *(Disappears.)*

*MARGARITA kneels before the seven-branched candle and anoints herself with the cream. She sings.*

## THE CREAM

MARGARITA: I am alone,

I take the cream.
It flows around me
as I dream.
My body fills
I feel I might
raise life tonight.

As I rise
I know I can
break the chain
that fetters man,
crush these walls
that prison me,
set me free!

*She unclasps her robe which falls away in one movement. She is naked.*

I am the woman in the moon.
I am the mother of earth.
I am the witch upon a broom.
I bring birth.

*She ascends to B.*

I am the Lady of the Lake.
I am the Queen of Strife.
I call the tide, I raise hell,
I bring life.

*She ascends to A.*

The Star of the Dawn,
I bring light.
I fly for ever above.
I am Eve, I am she
who ate of the Tree,
the Madonna with Child,
I bring love.

*Fade to black. Light discovers BORIS seated in D. As he speaks, he builds a tower of letter-bricks, spelling "COMPLACENCY".*

BORIS: I am so lucky. My life is rich. There's nothing I lack. Respected, successful, industrious, relaxed, I must be the perfect example of the satisfied citizen. And what is the source of my sufficiency? My wife. I look at her and I sometimes find myself almost believing in Providence! My friends never cease to compliment me. She is my just reward: beautiful, clever, in her prime, and married to me.

*MARGARITA appears on A, robed in white.*

MARGARITA: I've never loved you. I've lived a lie for ten years. I love someone else, far superior to you. Forget me as quickly as you can. I am leaving you for ever.

*Music as BORIS yells and MARGARITA walks down to B.*

BORIS: *(Demolishing the tower.)* Bitch! Whore! Tart! Liar!

*His light fades. On B two CLERKS are seated at the table with typewriters. A sign in front of them bears the bold title "BUREAUCRACY". The CLERKS type.*

1 CLERK: Come in.

2 CLERK: Wait there.

1 CLERK: Have you a card?

2 CLERK: Fill in the form in triplicate.

1 CLERK: In triplicate, in triplicate!

MARGARITA: I'm looking for a man.

2 CLERK: What's his number?

MARGARITA: I don't know.

1 CLERK: She doesn't know.

2 CLERK: Delete section A.

MARGARITA: He used to live in a basement flat.

1 CLERK: Where and when?

2 CLERK: Postal code?

MARGARITA: I'm not sure.

1 CLERK: She isn't sure.

2 CLERK: Delete section B.

MARGARITA: I used to go there by instinct.

1 CLERK: Do you have a Sanity Certificate?

MARGARITA: I love him.

2 CLERK: Married or single?

MARGARITA: Married, but not to him.

1 CLERK: Are you registered?

MARGARITA: What as?

2 CLERK: Adulteress –

1 CLERK: Nymphomaniac –

2 CLERK: Or prostitute?

MARGARITA: None of them.

1 CLERK: Delete section C.

MARGARITA: This man is my life!

2 CLERK: What's the time?

1 CLERK: Two minutes to one.

BOTH: Lunch!

*They stop typing and chatter.*

CLERKS: *(Alternate.)* So she told me, she did.
   – I don't believe it!
   – That's what *she* said.
   – She didn't!
   – So *I* told *her*.
   – And what did she say?
   – She said she wouldn't.
   – She didn't!
   – I tell you I couldn't believe it myself!
   – And you know what she said to me?
   – She said she told you.
   – She said she told me.
   – That's what *I* said.
   – You didn't!
   – And what did *she* say?
   – She said she wouldn't.
   – She did not!
   – I tell you I couldn't believe it myself.
   – What's the time?
   – Two minutes to two.
   – Back to work.

*They resume typing.*

MARGARITA: He wrote a book.

1 CLERK: Name and length.

2 CLERK: How many words?

MARGARITA: He destroyed it.

1 CLERK: Auto-destructed.

2 CLERK: Delete section D.

MARGARITA: It was reviewed.

1 CLERK: When was it published?

MARGARITA: It wasn't.

2 CLERK: If it was not published, how could it be reviewed?

MARGARITA: It was reviewed *before* it was published.

1 CLERK: Not possible.

2 CLERK: Not acceptable.

1 CLERK: What's the time?

2 CLERK: Two minutes to five.

BOTH: Finish! *(They pack up.)*

MARGARITA: The critics were Latunsky, Arimanova, Mstislav Lavrovich and Lapshennikova. Their names are seared in my heart because I wish to destroy them!

1 CLERK: I'm sorry.

2 CLERK: Got to go.

1 CLERK: Lock up.

2 CLERK: Clock out.

MARGARITA: *(With sudden power.)* You can't move!

*The CLERKS freeze.*

1 CLERK: I'm stuck to the floor!

2 CLERK: Glued to the chair!

MARGARITA: Give me a note of authority to take to the Propaganda Bureau. Then I'll let you go.

*Helpless the first CLERK starts to type the note. Music.*

CLERKS: *(Alternate.)* I hope you realize
- that by doing this
- we are forfeiting
- our usefulness
- to the system.
- We will be sacked
- as emotionally unstable
- imprecise time-keepers.
- The machine will seize up.
- We're ruined!

*MARGARITA snatches the note and confronts the SECURITY GUARD on the steps down to C. The GUARD wears grey uniform with black belt and cap. He carries a "lollipop" traffic sign, boldly inscribed "SECURITY".*

GUARD: Now what's all this?

MARGARITA: *(Showing note.)* I have a note of authority.

GUARD: *(Screws it up.)* No you haven't.

MARGARITA: I have permission.

GUARD: Not with me you haven't.

MARGARITA: I have to see the critics.

GUARD: It's more than my job's worth.

MARGARITA: Let me pass or you'll regret it!

GUARD: You can't get round me.

MARGARITA: *(With power.)* Your right arm is dead!

GUARD: *(Maimed.)* Bloody hell!

MARGARITA: Your left arm too!

GUARD: What are you doing!

MARGARITA: Your left leg.

GUARD: It's gone!

MARGARITA: So has your right!

*MARGARITA steps over the GUARD and proceeds down to C.*

GUARD: *(Fading.)* You won't get away with this! They'll catch up with you, you wait and see! I'm crippled. I can't move…

*At the table on C, sit the four CRITICS. A sign in front of them boldly proclaims "CENSORSHIP".*

MARGARITA: Good evening comrades!

1 CRITIC: Who is this?

2 CRITIC: What's happening?

MARGARITA: You destroyed the Master.

3 CRITIC: She's drunk!

4 CRITIC: She's a fanatic!

MARGARITA: You reviewed his book before it was published. That book was his life!

1 CRITIC: We have to protect our institutions from corruption.

2 CRITIC: We have no personal feelings for or against this writer.

3 CRITIC: His book was deemed to be dangerous to the state.

4 CRITIC: He had to be suppressed.

MARGARITA: *Why?*

ALL FOUR: He wrote lies.

1 CRITIC: He made out there was corruption within our ranks.

2 CRITIC: Now we all know if a structure is corrupt, it cannot stand.

3 CRITIC: And our structure is firm.

4 CRITIC: It stands proud and strong.

1 CRITIC: So it cannot be corrupt.

2 CRITIC: And so the book is lies.

MARGARITA: He wrote the *truth*: that all men are good!

ALL FOUR: As a unit they *are* good.

MARGARITA: As individuals.

1 CRITIC: Oh no.

2 CRITIC: Not so.

3 CRITIC: As individuals –

4 CRITIC: We are nothing.

MARGARITA: I looked at each head as it wagged on a stalk.
    The lips pronounce, and the tongues, they talk.
    Alone we are free; as one we are none.
    The curse is on *you*! I cried to each one.

1 CRITIC: What's she doing?

2 CRITIC: What's that smell?

3 CRITIC: Paraffin!

4 CRITIC: Stop her!

1 CRITIC: This building is filled with priceless manuscripts!

*Music. Flames.*

MARGARITA: Manuscripts don't burn! He set fire to his book but the truth wouldn't burn! Only lies burn! The truth is set free! *Fiat Lux!*

*BANG! Blackout.*

*Through dim smoke, an endless stream of sedated psychiatric patients issues from the base of the Tower, crawling like ants. They wear grey dressing-gowns and carry night-lights. They are the BALL GUESTS. They spread across D, shuffling around STRAVINSKY who stands on the block in a grey gown. A placard round his neck says "SEDATION".*

*MARGARITA wanders in a follow-spot among the GUESTS, looking for the MASTER.*

STRAVINSKY: I can't help you. I've lost the files. We're full to bursting, sleeping three to a bed and spilling into the corridors. Never had such an influx. It's the strain; I can't take it. *(Swallows pills.)* They bundle them in by the truckload. Half of them are as sane as you and me; just been knocked over by events. And I can't let them out without completing the treatment, and I can't complete the treatment because there's too bloody many of them. Also I've lost the files, you understand. So I haven't a clue which one is which! *(Takes more pills.)* And when I complain, the authorities tell me I'm right! I'm not meant to attend to each one individually because that's precisely what they're in for: hyperindividualism! I just have to lump them as one in a collective mass. Numb the skull and drain the brain. That's the routine. They're down there if you want to shop around. If you ask me, it's not a science any more, it's cabbage cultivation. *(More pills.)* Have a good look. See if you can spot him. They're all alike to me…

*WOLAND, cloaked and hooded, looms on A. BEHEMOTH, AZAZELLO and HELLA perch like vultures on A, B and C. WOLAND sings softly.*

## LOOK AROUND

WOLAND: Look around.

    Each guest
    is waiting
    to be addressed.
    Look around.
    Bid them all
    welcome
    to the Ball.
    As they lean or lie
    as they breathe and sigh,
    their lives crawl by.

BEHEMOTH: Psst!

AZAZELLO: Margarita.

HELLA: Your Majesty.

AZAZELLO: The guests for the Ball.

BEHEMOTH: They're arriving.

HELLA: You have to greet them.

*MARGARITA is drawn up the steps.*

WOLAND: Look around.
    Move on,
    don't linger.
    You have won.
    Let revenge
    be sweet
    as they fall
    at your feet.
    As they lean or lie,
    as they breathe and sigh,
    their lives crawl by.

MARGARITA: What do I do?

BEHEMOTH: Just smile.

HELLA: Don't let them see that you're frightened.

AZAZELLO: Or that you favour one more than another.

BEHEMOTH: Be charmed, be delighted.

HELLA: It will last for ages. You'll be terribly depressed.

*The ever-moving stream of GUESTS begins to climb the steps to be introduced one by one to MARGARITA on B. The GUESTS ascend and descend, bleary and drugged. Each bows and kisses MARGARITA's foot and returns to join the end of the queue snaking in dim light round and up the Tower. The GUESTS carry or trail broken sin-signs – "COMPLACENCY", "BUREAUCRACY" etc. JUDAS has "CORRUPTION". PILATE has "COWARDICE".*

WOLAND: Look around.

The moon

is full.

It's coming soon.

Look around

for your man

and raise him

if you can.

Does he lean or lie?

Does he breathe and sigh

as life crawls by?

*The theme becomes jaunty as GUESTS with placards come before MARGARITA. The DEMONS' words are amplified and childlike. MARGARITA preserves an impartial dignity, fighting waves of tiredness as the introductions go on and on.*

DEMONS: *(For BORIS MIKHAILOVICH/"COMPLACENCY".)*

Here is a man who thought he was safe,

sufficient unto the day

that his wife rebelled and left him.

His life is ebbing away.

MARGARITA: You are welcome to the Ball.

DEMONS: *(For CLERK/"BUREAUCRACY".)*

Meet the Clerk who stuck to the clock,

strictly rationed her chatter.

One day she contravened the rules.

Now she's mad as a hatter.

MARGARITA: You are welcome to the Ball.

DEMONS: *(For GUARD/"SECURITY".)*
> Here is a sad Security Guard.
> He trusted his physique;
> till it all fell down and he lost his job.
> He's far to weak to speak.

MARGARITA: You are welcome to the Ball.

DEMONS: *(For CRITIC/"CENSORSHIP".)*
> Here is a Critic. She wrote reviews.
> Her words she never did mince;
> till one day someone answered back.
> She's not been heard of since.

MARGARITA: You are welcome to the Ball.

DEMONS: *(For STRAVINSKY/"SEDATION".)*
> Stravinsky ran the hospital.
> It made him so depressed.
> He swallowed a tablet, then took two,
> and then took all the rest.

MARGARITA: You are welcome to the Ball.

DEMONS: *(For NURSE.)*
> The Doctor had a little Nurse –
> a sorry tale to tell.
> For every pill the doctor took,
> the Nurse took one as well.

MARGARITA: You are welcome to the Ball.

DEMONS: *(For JUDAS/"CORRUPTION".)*
> Friends are worth their weight in gold –
> and overstatement this.
> All Judas got was thirty silver
> pieces and a kiss.

MARGARITA: You are welcome to the Ball.

DEMONS: *(For PILATE/"COWARDICE".)*
> Truth was Pilate's problem.
> How it made his temples throb!
> He washed his hands of it and kept

his head-ache and his job.

MARGARITA: You are welcome to the Ball.

DEMONS: *(For BEZDOMNY.)*

Round and round we seem to go
and then from side to side.
Is this a pilgrimage or are we
just here for the ride?

MARGARITA: You are welcome to the Ball.

DEMONS: *(For BORIS.)*

Here is a man who thought he was safe…

*The process repeats till MARGARITA is collapsing with tiredness. Finally:*

WOLAND: It is time.

*The GUESTS stop dead. A clock strikes twelve. Rumbling sound as of an earthquake. Explosion of music and light. WOLAND revealed on A, in satanic majesty. The DEMONS hurl crimson rolls of cloth from A, B and C, like tongues of flame. The Tower seems to be falling. The GUESTS scream and try to escape, clambering in panic up the girders.*

WOLAND: Look around. The Ball is reeling
and the Master's confined.
Deaf he cannot hear. He cannot see.
He is blind.
Sins are closing in, but lady
you can survive.
You have to resurrect him
if you want him alive!

MARGARITA: *(Sings with WOLAND.)*

I see the Ball is reeling
and the Master's confined.
Deaf he cannot hear. He cannot see.
He is blind.
Sins are closing in, but I know
I can survive.
I have to resurrect him
if I want him alive!

247

*Instrumental section. "The Ball" theme wrestles with "The Tower of State" theme. Finally the struggle is over. MARGARITA collapses. WOLAND sings as the GUESTS pick themselves up and drift away.*

WOLAND: Look around.

> They go.
> It's over.
> Be it so.
> See them all
> weary and worn.
> They don't know they're born.
> They have eyes to see
> but they daren't see me.
> So let it be.

*(As his light fades, he whispers.)* Do you believe in magic? Do you believe in the Power of Good?

*Light remains on MARGARITA. The rest is black. Slowly the light on A returns. In place of WOLAND, stands the MASTER, in grey dressing-gown, head bowed. MARGARITA looks up, rises and slowly walks up the steps towards him. Soft organ reprise of Bach's "O Sacred Head". MATTHEW dimly lit on D.*

MATTHEW: About daybreak on the Sunday, Mary of Magdala came to the tomb. It was empty. There was an earthquake. Suddenly he was there. He said: Why do you seek the living among the dead? Know that I am risen. For lo I am with you always, even unto the end of the world.

*His light fades as she reaches the MASTER. He does not look up. Light comes up on PILATE on B. His SECRETARY is beside him. They wear grey Roman clothes.*

SECRETARY: Have you slept sir?

PILATE: A little.

SECRETARY: The storm was unprecedented, surpassing all known records. I have an account of damage to public property, also a flood report sir.

PILATE: I had such a dream.

SECRETARY: Sir?

PILATE: I was walking along a path of light to the moon. Beside me was my dog, and the vagrant philospher Ha-Notsri.

SECRETARY: Should I arrange an interpretation sir?

PILATE: We debated as we walked. We argued intensely. We disagreed absolutely. The execution of course had been a mistake. It couldn't have happened because the man was walking beside me.

SECRETARY: I have the report of the execution sir.

PILATE: Which is the greater sin: corruption or cowardice? I maintained the former, which, however disguised, could never be other than destructive and immoral. He argued for the latter, despite my protestation that the alleged sin has many faces, some of which, given the circumstances, could be deemed positively virtuous. I cited expediency, moderation, even wisdom, as synonyms for cowardice. I drew his attention to my part in his trial. I maintained that my action was honourable and courageous in that my duty as Procurator outweighed any personal feelings I held for the man himself. I had acted in the interest of law and order and good government, and this I argued could not possibly be construed as cowardice. The debate of course was pure hypothesis, and therefore unimpassioned, the execution never having taken place. *(Pause.)*

SECRETARY: It appears sir, that the victims had all expired by mid-day, and the guard contingent was dismissed as the storm broke.

PILATE: Corruption, on the other hand, is evil whichever way it faces. *(Pause.)*

SECRETARY: When the relief contingent came to clear the gibbets, the body of Ha-Notsri sir, had disappeared. The commander wishes to be informed as to how seriously he should regard this irregularity sir.

PILATE: Send a man to Caiaphas.

SECRETARY: Sir?

PILATE: Ask the High Priest if he would be so good as to visit me this evening.

*Cross-fade to C. JUDAS OF KARIOTH dimly lit.*

JUDAS: Nisa...? I'm here... Come on you little minx, I know you're hiding... I've got something for you... *(Indicates bag of money.)* Nisa... Don't be shy... *(Laughs.)* I know you're there...

MURIBELLUM: *(In the shadows.)* Judas of Karioth?

JUDAS: *(Gasps.)*

MURIBELLUM: Are you alone?

JUDAS: *(Terrified.)* I'm waiting for my girl. We agreed to meet here.

MURIBELLUM: How much did you get?

JUDAS: What do you mean?

MURIBELLUM: From the High Priest.

JUDAS: Thirty tetradrachmas. Here, you can have it –

*He tries to run. MURIBELLUM slits his throat. Cut to B. CAIAPHAS is with PILATE and the SECRETARY.*

PILATE: It was good of you to spare me your time High Priest.

CAIAPHAS: I trust nothing is amiss Procurator.

PILATE: I won't keep you. *(Pause.)*

SECRETARY: Do you wish me to take notes sir?

PILATE: Every word. *(Pause.)*

CAIAPHAS: I gather one of the bodies was stolen.

PILATE: Is that so?

CAIAPHAS: The man Ha-Notsri. I have information to the effect that it was removed illegally by an ex-tax-collector, a Levite.

PILATE: Name of Matthew.

CAIAPHAS: You know this?

PILATE: I am kept informed.

CAIAPHAS: It seems he has lodged the body in the shack of a gardener in Bethphagy. The Sanhedrin recommends that measures be taken –

PILATE: I think we can leave the gardener to his own affairs High Priest.

CAIAPHAS: The deceased has followers.

PILATE: So I am told.

CAIAPHAS: They may use the disappearance of the body for the treasonable promotion of a messianic heresy.

PILATE: They may also seek to discredit you High Priest, with the charge of corruption: that you bribed an informer to betray the man.

CAIAPHAS: The Sanhedrin is above corruption.

PILATE: They plan to kill the informer and return the thirty tetradrachmas to you with a public note.

CAIAPHAS: They should be closely watched.

PILATE: That's not necessary.

CAIAPHAS: A scandal could inflame the people Procurator.

PILATE: Their plans have been forestalled. *(Gives him a purse of money.)* In the interest of good government, we will close the matter, though of course it has to remain on record. It's complete: thirty pieces. But take care, his blood is on it. *(Pause.)*

CAIAPHAS: The Sanhedrin will be grateful for your prompt action Procurator.

PILATE: *(To SECRETARY.)* Close the book.

*Cross-fade to D. BEZDOMNY seated on the block as at the beginning of the play.*

BEZDOMNY: Sometimes I come here when the moon is full. We sat here all those years ago, the Chairman and I. I was nervous, impressionable, arrogant with regard to my writing. I recall my breakdown, how I lost control: the hallucinations, my susceptibility to hypnosis. I recall the devotion extended to me by the staff of the clinic; the stranger who came to see me and told me of his book – he never existed! There was no mention of him in the files! I can reflect how lucky I have been to recover so completely. I can recall others less fortunate than I: the critic Latunsky who threw himself off a bridge; the architect Boris Mikhailovich, who lost control when his wife committed suicide. He had everything to look forward to. She was carrying his child. *(Pause.)* I come here when my head aches, to reflect on these things. It creeps up behind the eye: a clot of pain. There's no cure. I come here with my little bag, to sit it out.

*WOLAND has descended from A, dressed as the Professor, as in the first scene.*

WOLAND: May I join you? *(Sits.)* Forgive me, I'm intruding.

BEZDOMNY: I have a head-ache.

WOLAND: Extraordinary.

BEZDOMNY: It's quite commonplace.

WOLAND: Can you explain it?

BEZDOMNY: I only wish for it to go away.

WOLAND: It has a will of its own?

BEZDOMNY: It will pass.

WOLAND: What caused it?

BEZDOMNY: Stress.

WOLAND: Blinkers.

BEZDOMNY: I'm happy with my life. I don't wish it to be disrupted.

WOLAND: You're wearing blinkers.

BEZDOMNY: I'm a writer.

WOLAND: Of what?

BEZDOMNY: Reviews, essays, commentaries.

WOLAND: Nothing original.

BEZDOMNY: I'm writing a book disproving the existence of Jesus Christ.

WOLAND: When will you finish it?

BEZDOMNY: *(Shrugs.)* Next year.

WOLAND: You'll be dead.

BEZDOMNY: I've completely recovered –

WOLAND: Cancer of the liver. You have it already. Make the most of what is left. Throw a party, take poison. Depart from this world to the sound of violins and the drunken happiness of loving friends.

BEZDOMNY: I don't accept that.

WOLAND: *(Going.)* Otherwise you will die in the early morning of the 9th of March in ward number four of the First Moscow City Hospital.

*Cross-fade to B. PILATE is walking with YESHUA in a shaft of moonlight: PILATE in grey toga, YESHUA in white robe, crowned with white roses.*

PILATE: Expediency, moderation, even wisdom…

YESHUA: Excuses Procurator.

PILATE: You were never in the business of government Ha-Notsri.

YESHUA: You're hiding your conscience.

PILATE: I can't afford a conscience.

YESHUA: Your sin lingers on. You will live with it for ever.

PILATE: Perpetual debate is the essence of life.

YESHUA: Perpetual denial.

PILATE: Call it what you like. As long as we keep talking –

YESHUA: The pain is avoided.

PILATE: There was no pain.

YESHUA: You could have spared me.

PILATE: It never happened.

YESHUA: I have the marks of the nails.

PILATE: We established that the execution never took place.

YESHUA: It is believed.

PILATE: *(Smiling.)* Tax-collectors don't make reliable historians.

*Cross-fade to D. BEZDOMNY's head is splitting. As he speaks, he takes from his bag, a syringe, ampoule and swabs. He prepares his arm.*

BEZDOMNY: Man has mastered his emotions. We have an answer for everything. Wonderment is ignorance. There is no time for it. I come here with my little bag to reflect on this, and to carry out my doctor's instructions. I accept that there are forces on either side, but we are not at liberty, in a sane society, to consider them. The present is our only concern, the cross-flow of these forces. We may examine the synthesis in which we live and move. To look beyond that is wrong. *(He injects himself.)*

*His light dims as he leans forward, eyes closed. Light comes up on B. PILATE and YESHUA walk and speak in slow motion as BEZDOMNY's sedation takes effect.*

PILATE: Say it never took place.

YESHUA: *(Smiling.)* It never took place.

PILATE: Will you swear it?

YESHUA: I swear it never took place. It was purely your imagination.

PILATE: That is all I need to know…

*Their beam of light fades. BEZDOMNY's light remains dim. Light discovers MARGARITA in red robe on A.*

## THE TWELVE

MARGARITA: When the moon breaks
and light streams
and the head aches
and it seems
that the night is flooding
black upon red
and hell arises
around your bed,
then close your eyes
to evil and good
and all will end
as it should.

When the blizzard swirls
and the wind cries
and the world is riven
with sighs
of the lame and hungry
homeless and cold
who slip and stagger
and lose their hold,
then shut out the sound
and blot out the sight
and all will be ended
aright.

*The rhythm changes as the COMPANY is discovered dimly in the storm, grey-uniformed, motionless, in marching attitude in a long line up all the steps and platforms towards A, YESHUA in white, leading. The sky glows red.*

COMPANY: There's an army of Twelve.

They battle the storm.
They challenge the wind
and the roaring sky.
They're marching as one.
They aid none at all.
Come follow or fall
is the cry.

So march the Twelve
the army of man.
The banner unfurled
is brave, blood-red.
The weak will fall,
the waverers die.
And Christ in white
is striding ahead!

*The army fades.*

MARGARITA: And a homeless dog,
hungry and blind

follows, is left
behind.
So fall to the wind
and yield to the snow.
Shut out the light
the pain will go.
Cover your eyes.
The truth is a lie.
And all will end
bye and bye.

*Her light fades. BEZDOMNY's light fades. Blackout.*
*End of the Play.*

WWW.OBERONBOOKS.COM

www.ingramcontent.com/pod-product-compliance
Ingram Content Group UK Ltd.
Pitfield, Milton Keynes, MK11 3LW, UK
UKHW020738280225
455688UK00013B/731